2012 COPO CAMARO

The Chevy Performance Team Unleashes a Legend

By Jeffrey K. Leestma and the Editors of *Automobile Quarterly*

2012 COPO CAMARO

The Chevy Performance Team Unleashes a Legend

By Jeffrey K. Leestma

Publisher: Kaye Bowles-Durnell

Managing Editor: John Durnell

Art Director: Dan Bulleit

Co-Designer: Tim Lee

Photo Research: Deb Murphy

ISBN: 978-1-59613-076-0

(812) 948-AUTO (2886)
Toll Free (866) 838-AUTO (2886)
www.autoquarterly.com
800 East 8th Street, New Albany, IN 47150

Printed in the United States of America

CONTENTS

FOREWORD / Jim Campbell 4

Chapter 1 THE COPO LEGACY 6

Chapter 2 CAMARO HERITAGE 14

Chapter 3 RACING CAMAROS 30

Chapter 4 GEN FIVE CAMARO 40

Chapter 5 COPO IS REBORN 50

Chapter 6 PROOF-OF-CONCEPT 62

Chapter 7 COPO BUILD 74

Chapter 8 COPO MARKETING 94

Chapter 9 THE ENTHUSIASTS 108

Chapter 10 COPO AT SPEED 150

Appendix One: COPO CAMARO SPECIFICATIONS 160

Appendix Two: CAMARO GENERATIONS 164

Acknowledgements 170

8

FOREWORD

"The 1969 COPO Camaros were created using a kind of 'insider's knowledge' and a 'break-the-rules' approach to building some of the fastest, most famous street and strip machines of all time. Chevrolet is breaking the rules again by bringing back the COPO Camaro."

Jim Campbell, U.S. VP, Chevrolet Performance Vehicles and Motorsports

From the brand's very beginning in 1911, the name Chevrolet has stood for racing and outstanding automotive performance. It's no secret why the brand's founder, Billy Durant, chose that name. Louis Chevrolet, a Swiss-born Frenchman who emigrated to the United States, raced his entire life, first on bicycles as a young man, and then piloting some of the fastest race cars in the early 20th Century. He then went on to construct some of the fastest cars that dominated racing circuits from coast to coast. Louis Chevrolet was one of America's original racing "superstars." He just wanted to go fast. Then, as now, the name Chevrolet is synonymous with performance.

Since its introduction in late 1966, the Chevrolet Camaro has captured the hearts and imaginations of those looking for sporty performance. Be it on the street, track or strip, Camaro has been a consistent and dominant American racing icon for nearly half a century. Always representing the perfect balance between performance and style, it's no wonder that Camaro has become "America's muscle car." And one of the greatest Camaros of all time was the 1969 Central Office Production Order (COPO) Camaro.

The COPO acronym has the ability to raise adrenalin levels to new heights. At car auctions, these four letters are guaranteed to bring bidding to a frenzy. No doubt some of the appeal comes from the fact that the 1969 COPO Camaros were created using a kind of "insider's knowledge" and a "break-the-rules" approach to building some of the fastest, most famous street and strip machines of all time.

Chevrolet is breaking the rules again by bringing back the COPO Camaro. This time, the 2012 COPO Camaro is designed to give Stock and Super Stock competitors a "straight-from-the-factory" race car. Taking a page from the original COPO playbook, the new COPO Camaros are once again created outside the normal ordering process. Participating Chevy dealers were required to custom order the vehicle for their customers "off line," separate from the other vehicles they might order. In this way, the original Central Office Production Order system was authentically recreated.

This book commemorates the revival of the world-famous COPO Camaro. It will give you a behind-the-scenes look at its development and its creation. In any successful project, especially in racing, it takes an intensely passionate team. Those are precisely the kind of people who made the COPO Camaro a reality.

This is a "must have" book for every Chevrolet, Camaro and COPO enthusiast. Join me in celebrating the continuation of one of the most successful performance stories of all time.

COPO is alive and well!

See you in the Winner's Circle!

Jim Campbell

Jim Campbell
U.S.Vice President,
Chevrolet Performance Vehicles and Motorsports

CHAPTER ONE: **THE COPO LEGACY**

"COPO was a great way to get a more relevant product in the hands of amateur racers."

Mark Kent, Director, Chevy Racing

In the world of muscle cars, GM's Central Office Production Order system, or COPO, is revered among collectors and has taken on nearly mythical proportions. When a COPO Camaro crosses the auction block (even a well-executed COPO clone), the bidding paddles wave with increased fervor.

What has now assumed legendary status among Camaro aficionados began quite modestly as a way for fleet buyers to order customized vehicles. The Central Office Production Order was the antithesis of the Regular Production Order, or RPO, and gave large volume buyers such as rental car companies, police departments and taxi operators a way to special-order cars that would meet their particular needs. A taxi fleet operator, for example, might request a car with a heavy-duty suspension or a particular engine, or the ability to delete certain items. These choices were unavailable to dealers and the general public.

But there were monster-motor Camaros running loose on the streets well before Chevy hot-rodders tapped into the COPO system to build them in-house.

When the first-generation Camaro was introduced for the 1967 model year, it didn't take long for a few enterprising and performance-minded Chevrolet dealers like Gibb, Yenko, Nickey, Thomas, Dana, Baldwin and Berger, to name a few, to install the most powerful engine possible. That engine, of course, was the mighty Chevy 427 big block. There was good reason why the 427-cubic-inch engine was not available in the Camaro; GM was under a self-imposed restriction that Camaro engines not exceed 400 cubic inches, for fear that the Camaro might out-perform Chevrolet's iconic sports car, the Corvette, if it carried the same motor.

Undeterred, these dealers sourced 427 engines from Chevy as parts counter crate motors, which was a very expensive option, or in some rare cases, from donor Corvettes or full-size Chevrolets. The

Facing page: The '69 COPO Camaro in all its subdued glory. The plain-looking COPO, replete with the famous "dog dish" hubcaps, gave no outward appearance of the power that lurked within.

Above: Dealer Don Yenko was one of a handful of Chevy dealers stuffing big block motors into Chevelles, Chevy IIs and Camaros.

Left: The famed Nickey Camaros were identified simply by the Nickey logo with the red, backward 'K.'

Above: The Baldwin Motion Camaros looked more aggressive in appearance than other high-performance Camaros, and had the power to back up the look.

Right: Camaros lined up in the Yenko lot awaiting modification.

results were Camaros that dominated the street and strip.

Perhaps the most well known today of the super Camaros are the ones created by Chevy dealer Don Yenko of Canonsburg, Pennsylvania. He began by ordering stock Camaro SS models from the factory, which were equipped with 396-cubic-inch engines, and then transplanting the big 427.

The Yenko Camaros were very fast. Often called a wolf in sheep's clothing, the Yenko Camaros outward appearance did not look much different than a stock SS,

with the exception of the unique Yenko stripe and "sYc" logo (which stood for Yenko Super Car). Yenko built an estimated 50 super Camaros in 1967 and another, smaller batch, in 1968. The cars were expensive to build and few customers were willing to spend well more than twice what a normal Camaro cost. Those who could afford the Yenko Camaro, however, were rewarded with a neck-snapping ride and a solid investment.

Similarly, Nickey Chevrolet of Chicago was stuffing 427 big blocks into Camaros, as well as Chevelles and Chevy II Novas, with the help of aftermarket performance genius Bill Thomas. The Nickey conversions were so discreet, in fact, that the only way someone waiting at a red light could tell that they were about to get their doors blown off was the famous Nickey decal with the backward "K."

Baldwin Chevrolet in Long Island, New York, partnered with aftermarket speed shop Motion Performance, run by the legendary Joel Rosen, to create its own version of the super Camaro. The Baldwin Motion

Most Yenko Camaros started as SS models before they were modified. Ornamentation was kept to a minimum, making them as beautiful as they were fast.

Camaros, as they were called, were truly monsters to contend with, as they not only carried the 427 motor, but incredibly, Rosen shoe-horned the even bigger displacement Chevy 454 engine into the Camaro engine bay in the early '70s.

Dana Chevrolet of South Gate, California, and Berger Chevrolet of Grand Rapids, Michigan, were yet two more dealers cramming 427 big blocks into Camaros. The Dana Camaros were identifiable by the larger performance hoods and fatter tires, and for offering customers various levels of performance based on what they wanted to achieve and how much they could spend.

The Berger Camaros were less noticeable on the street, but equally potent. They were distinguished by a small chrome badge at the rear that simply stated "by

it, in other words, skirting the established RPO process. Some individuals in GM management, and surely plant management, realized these 427 engines were being installed outside the normal process, but looked the other way. This clearly added a sort of cloak-and-dagger image to COPO, a far cry from its original mundane purpose. Using the COPO system required two things: knowledge that the process even existed, and a GM insider who could give dealers access to it.

That access point, initially, was believed to be

Above left: The "sYc" logo stood for Yenko Super Car, and it was.

Above right: Performance Chevy dealer Don Yenko, right, and racer Dick Harrell at the track.

Berger." The original Berger cars are rare and highly collectible today. It should be noted that Berger is still selling Chevrolets to this day and still focused on performance.

By 1968, these few performance dealers learned that they could get the 427 motors installed in Camaros by the factory. They had discovered the Central Office Production Order.

"COPO was a great way to get a more relevant product in the hands of amateur racers," explains Chevy Director of Racing Mark Kent.

The original COPO system was somewhat secretive, as GM didn't want but just a handful of dealers using

none-other than Ed Cole, General Motors president in 1967. Cole, known as the father of the wildly successful Chevrolet small-block motor, had Chevrolet in his soul, having previously served as Chevy chief engineer in the '50s, then later promoted to Chevrolet Division general manager and a corporate vice president. It was no secret that Cole and Don Yenko were friends and the initial idea to use the COPO system to order performance variants was likely hatched between the two.

But once this handful of dealers got past the gatekeeper, Cole, the point person was Vince Piggins, at the

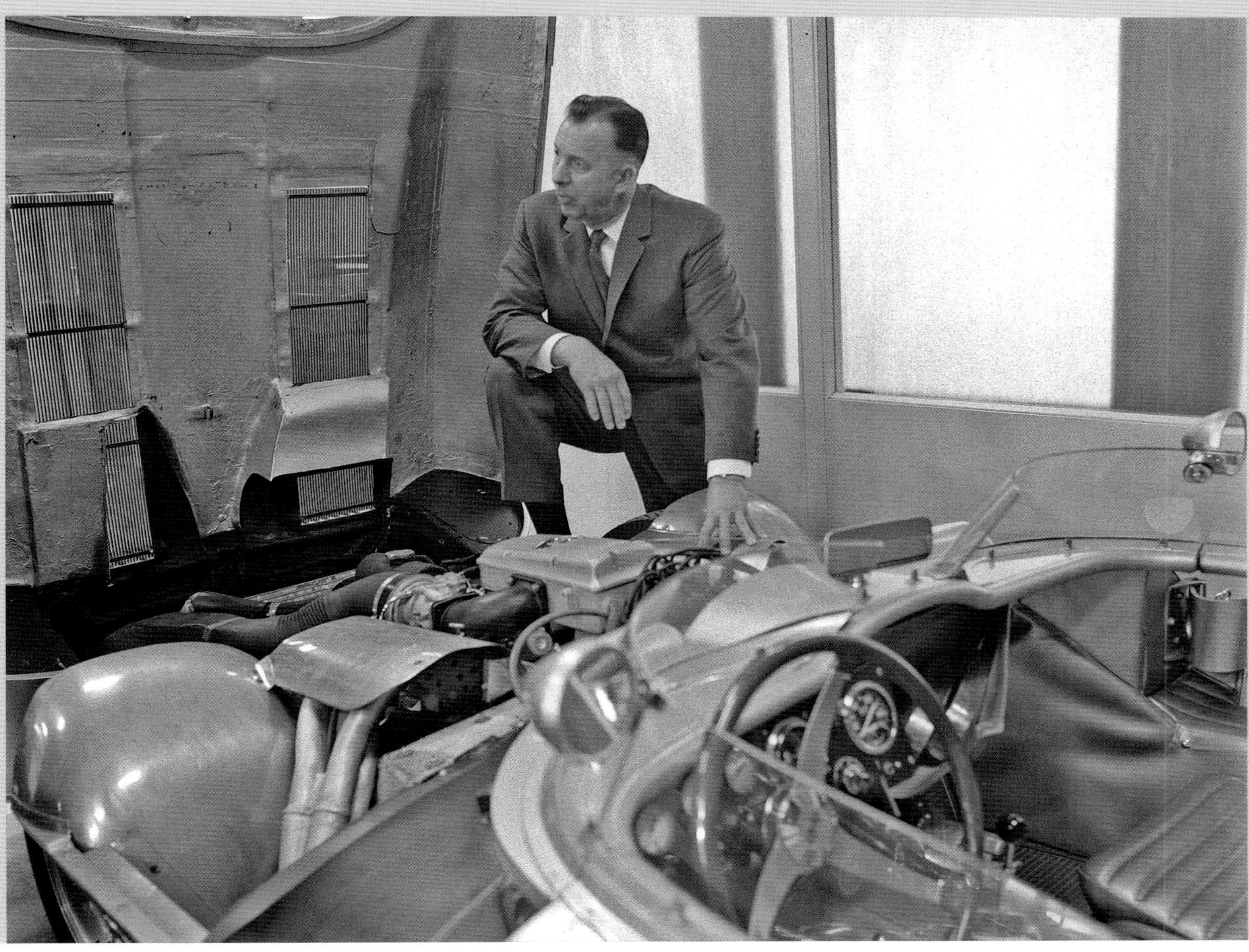

GM President and former Chevy Chief Engineer Ed Cole was "Mr. Chevrolet" in every sense, and it was his direct involvement that got the COPO Camaro project off the ground.

time Chevrolet's then-product promotions manager (and the so-called "father" of the Z28). His primary responsibility was promoting racing and performance vehicles. First enacted in 1957 and firmly re-stated in 1963, GM's official no-racing policy put the job descriptions of Piggins and others like him involved in performance into a sort of gray area.

Piggins figured that if GM was not going to officially support racing with a factory effort he would establish discreet relationships with a few privateers, making sure they had the parts and expertise necessary to put the Chevrolet bowtie in the winner's circle. Working at first with a select group of proven dealers such as Yenko, Piggins effectively nourished Chevy's performance image even as GM policy intended an opposite result.

Tweaking the COPO system to produce factory hot rods was a brilliant next step. It was an already established corporate process. It brought a modicum of coherence to what had been a free-wheeling adventure. And Piggins' tiny group of enthusiast dealers loved it because speed equipment was now factory-installed and backed by a GM warranty.

The first batch of COPO Camaros was unleashed to compete in National Hot Rod Association Stock and

Right: Two decades after the COPO Camaro debuted, the idea of installing big-block motors in Camaros, as evidenced by this April 1987 cover of *Muscle Car Review*, had achieved cult-like status. This issue carried the last interview with Don Yenko, who died in March that same year.

Below: The back end of a Baldwin Motion Camaro was a familiar sight to many drag racers.

DUAL COVERAGE:
'87 BUICK GRAND NATIONAL ROAD TEST
BUICK'S HOT NEW '87 GNX

MUSCLE
CAR REVIEW

FIRST PHOTOS

BIG BLOCK CAMAROS

IDENTIFICATION GUIDE · ZL-1 AND 427 COPOS · DON YENKO INTERVIEW
BIG BLOCK PERFORMANCE TUNING

More Muscle:
'70 CHALLENGER R/T · '69 MERCURY SPOILER II · '70 ... 4-4-2

Super Stock Eliminator classes. These Camaros carried the aluminum-block ZL1 motor, as opposed to the iron-block 427s that had been previously installed. But in order to be sanctioned for NHRA stock classes, Chevrolet needed to build at least 50 production, street-legal units.

In all, 69 of these factory COPO ZL1 Camaros were built. The first 50 were built to meet the NHRA requirement, all ordered by LaHarpe, Illinois, Chevy dealer Fred Gibb; the remaining 19 units went to buyers with deep

This 1969 COPO Camaro is as good as it gets: simply beautiful and extremely fast.

pockets. Today these are some of the most sought after of all the COPO Camaros built.

Among the most notable of the COPO options, of course, was the choice of engines. COPO order number 9561 installed the 427 L72 cast-iron motor. COPO number 9560 installed the incredible 427 ZL1, a Corvette-exclusive aluminum-block engine intended for NHRA drag racing. These engines came with a high price, however. Option 9560 added about $4,000 to the sticker at the time, roughly doubling the price of the car.

Most of the Yenko Camaros were also ordered with a COPO-only "sports car conversion" kit. Carrying COPO order code 9737, this package added E70x15 Goodyear Wide Tread GT tires mounted to 15-inch rally wheels, a 140-mph speedometer and a thicker stabilizer bar. Later COPO 9737 cars came with a center-mounted gas gauge and a factory-installed tachometer.

In 1968 and 1969, Chevy built nearly a thousand Camaros using the COPO system. These were mostly for the aforementioned aftermarket performance dealers using the L72 cast-iron engine. The 69 all-aluminum 427 ZL1 COPO Camaros simply re-wrote the history of American drag racing.

Sadly, at least for collectors and racers, the COPO program lasted only a few years. The COPO program was the victim of a perfect storm of events: the gas crisis, the auto industry's move toward reduced vehicle build complexity, in other words, less options and choices, and finally, increased government regulations and certifications.

"Over the years there have been many historical moments in Chevy racing, and COPO has been a part of that," says Kent.

For Chevrolet and Camaro lovers, the famed COPO program is the topic of never-ending nostalgic discussions, a remembrance of a golden era of performance gone by.

That is, until now.

The Hugger
327
FRONT E

CHAPTER TWO: **CAMARO HERITAGE**

"Camaro is for the owner who expects his personal tastes and action to be reflected in a clean, modern, and dynamic styling line and quick, sharply defined performance."

Chevrolet Passenger Car Engineering Features, 1967

Before there was a COPO Camaro, there had to be a Camaro.

From the beginning, Camaro was known for its sporting image. The Camaro was born to compete. And Camaro's first competition was the Ford Mustang.

In the early 1960s, Chevrolet had two small car offerings, the Corvair and the Chevy II. The Corvair was nothing short of revolutionary in the American market in 1960. Most notably, the car's engine was in the rear, the engine was air cooled, and it featured a unique four-wheel independent suspension. The only other car in the U.S. market in 1960 with a similar rear-engine, rear-drive layout that sold in volume was the Volkswagen Beetle.

The Beetle sold very well, with VW producing well over 700,000 units worldwide in 1960. But the Beetle was an aging, pre-war design, and despite its popularity and cult-status among young people at the time, its decline was inevitable.

The Corvair, however, was modern and sleek, and featured a kind of European-inspired styling that could be found nowhere else on the North American automotive landscape. And despite the Corvair's later tainted reputation, it was actually a well-engineered car and sold well, about 200,000 units a year.

At the time of the introduction of the Ford Mustang in 1964, Chevy offered the Chevy II, above, and the Corvair, left, in the compact segment of the market. Despite early confidence that these two cars combined could compete with the Mustang, Chevy soon realized a more direct competitor was needed.

This page: Early full-scale clay mock-ups already began to exhibit the iconic Camaro shape, with mainly proportional tweaks yet to be made.

The Chevy II was a more traditional vehicle, with a front, liquid-cooled engine and rear-wheel drive, with a solid rear axle. Its design was decidedly boxy and straightforward. Both the Corvair and the Chevy II were available in two-door, four-door, convertible and wagon configurations.

Across town, Ford was selling its popular Falcon model, also available in two-door, four-door, convertible and wagon styles. With Chevrolet bookending the Falcon with the sleek Corvair on the one side, and the more directly competitive Chevy II on the other, GM had nothing to worry about. That is, until April 17, 1964.

On that day, Ford unveiled to the public a new, sporty small car at the New York World's Fair. Though based mechanically on the Falcon, the Mustang looked nothing like the Falcon. The Mustang featured a long hood, short rear deck, and smooth sporty styling. The Mustang was available in two-door coupe and convertible styles (with a 2+2 fastback introduced a few months later). The Mustang struck an immediate chord with the public. Still, GM was not particularly worried. But when Mustang sales exceeded 100,000 units in just its first three months and about a million units in the first 18 months, GM and Chevrolet leadership knew they had to respond.

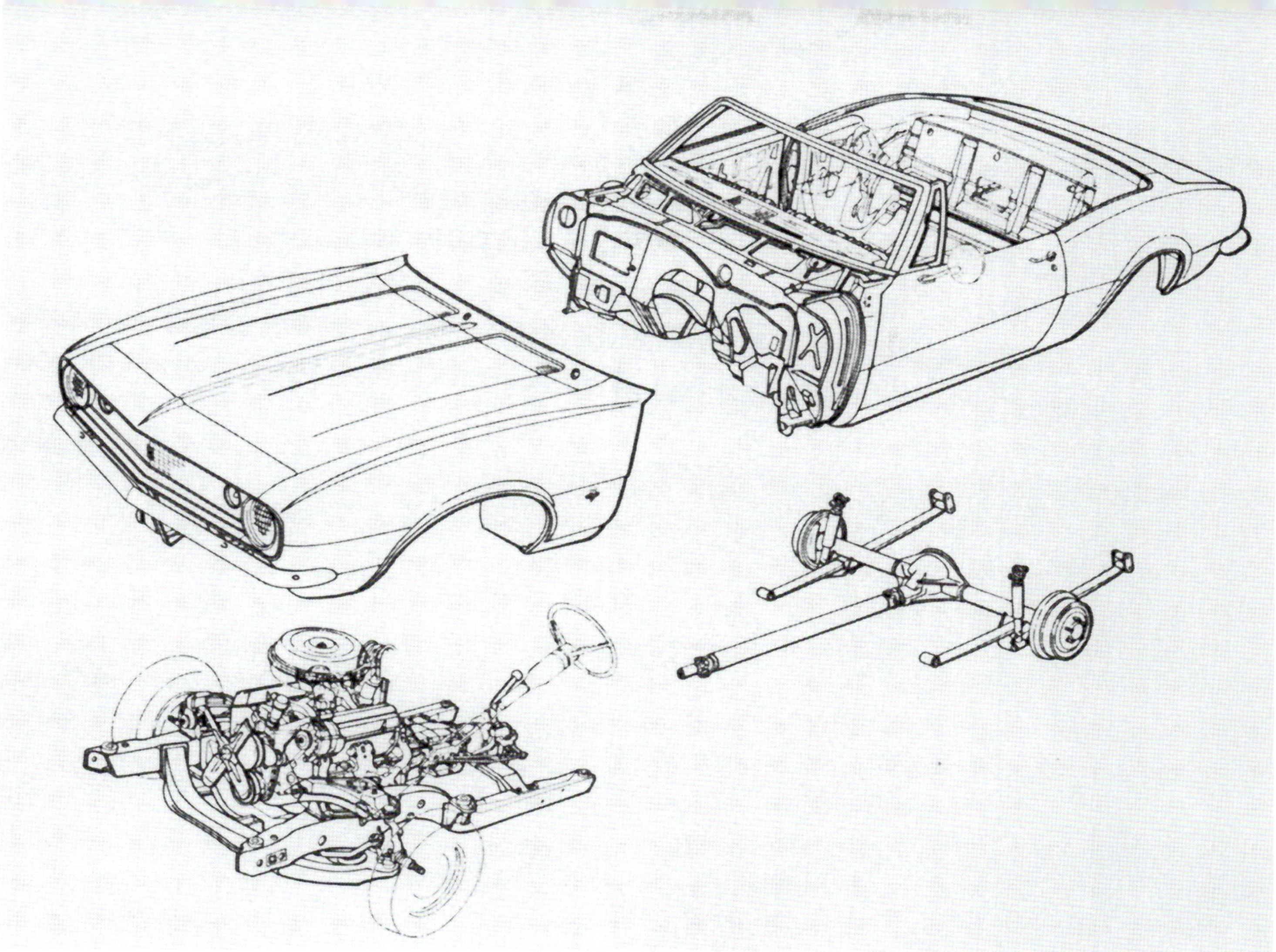

Above: In order to develop the Camaro in record time, Chevy engineers created a revolutionary separate front sub-frame, allowing the Camaro and the Chevy II to share front-end engineering, with unique unibodies from the firewall rearward.

Below: Despite being called a Nova, the 1964 Chevy II Super Nova concept provided the styling basis for the new Camaro.

Above: Even in the earliest stages of development, alternate body styles were considered, such as a convertible, which was wisely introduced, and a station wagon, which wisely, was not.

Right: This early clay rear treatment, which still carried the Panther nameplate, is actually a design that would be applied to the Camaro's cousin, the Pontiac Firebird, which was also introduced in 1967.

But how? With what vehicle? And how fast could it be developed?

The third-generation Chevy II was scheduled for the 1968 model year. Chevrolet managers knew they couldn't wait that long to respond to the Mustang, but by developing both cars simultaneously, they could hope to get the new car, as yet unnamed, into the market as a 1967 model. Moreover, GM knew that the new car would be available as a two-door sporty coupe only, whereas the Chevy II would continue with two-door and four-door versions (but no convertible or wagon).

The new car was code-named "Panther" for lack of a permanent name. For engineering purposes it was known as the F-body. GM designers and engineers knew that the 1964½ Mustang was not the target, but rather, a significantly freshened Mustang anticipated for the 1967 model year. (Mustang purists consider the first generation to be 1964½ to 1973, yet the 1967 model was a significantly changed vehicle, and larger than its predecessor.)

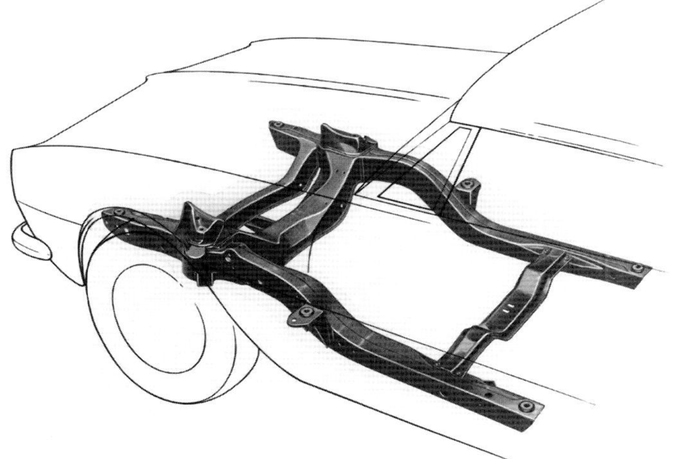

Above: Throughout the development of the Camaro, there was always a Ford Mustang nearby to be used for side-by-side comparisons.

Left: The unique Camaro front sub-frame.

GM stylists struggled with the F-body design, first as it translated from sketches and renderings to three-dimensional studies, and then from one clay model to the next. Not only did it need to look better than the Mustang, it had to be differentiated significantly from the Chevy II. There was always a Mustang nearby in the design studio to compare designs side-by-side. The new

Below: The June 1966 issue of *Mechanix Illustrated* showed a rendering of the new Camaro, still called Panther by the magazine. While the car in the rendering was not as curvaceous as the real Camaro, it was close enough to force Chevy to take action, prompting a national press conference with then-Chevy General Manager Elliott "Pete" Estes, to clear the air and correct errors of fact.

Right: When the Camaro was finally introduced to the press, Estes did so "with a bang."

car had to impress; there was no margin for error.

Engineers decided that instead of utilizing a full-length frame, as was the norm for the period, they would design a unique front sub-frame carrying the engine, transmission, and steering linkage. This sub-frame would then be connected to a unitized main body, giving the engineers the flexibility to develop the F-body and the Chevy II together and yet separately.

As early as 1965, the automotive press had begun to speculate about a Mustang-beater from Chevy, and the Panther name had actually been leaked to the media, not to mention a few spy photos of the disguised car under development. Needless to say, the anticipation of the new car was at a fever pitch, not the least of which was the trepidation that must have been felt at the Ford headquarters in Dearborn. While Ford relished the fact that they had gotten a head start and enjoyed several years without competition, they also must have realized

Left: This 1967 catalog photo was intended to convey the free-spirited nature of the new Camaro.

Below: This 1967 billboard for the new Camaro used few words, but still conveyed the youthful, sporty character of Chevrolet's new coupe.

that GM would respond with a great effort.

But while some of the information and speculation were correct, much of it was incorrect. Moreover, some automotive journalists were criticizing GM for taking so long, even though in reality GM was developing the car at a torrid pace. Some journalists even predicted that GM might not launch a new car at all.

Chevrolet had heard enough, and to clear the air a nationwide press conference took place on June 29, 1966. In what was perhaps the most elaborate telephone conference call in history up to that time, Chevy Public Relations connected journalists in 14 cities with microphones and speakers for a live question-and-answer session with Elliott "Pete" Estes, the newly-named Chevrolet general manager.

During this conference call, Estes updated the press about the status of the program, and in doing so, uttered the name "Camaro" for the first time. While there is no dispute about when the Camaro name was first mentioned in public, there remains a somewhat clouded mystery about the true origin of the name. Estes himself claimed that he came up with the name, while others say it was Chevy Merchandising Manager Bob Lund. Some believe it was the result of a corporation-wide solicitation of names from employees. Yet others claim that Camaro was part of a list of suggested names provided by Campbell-Ewald, Chevrolet's advertising agency at the time.

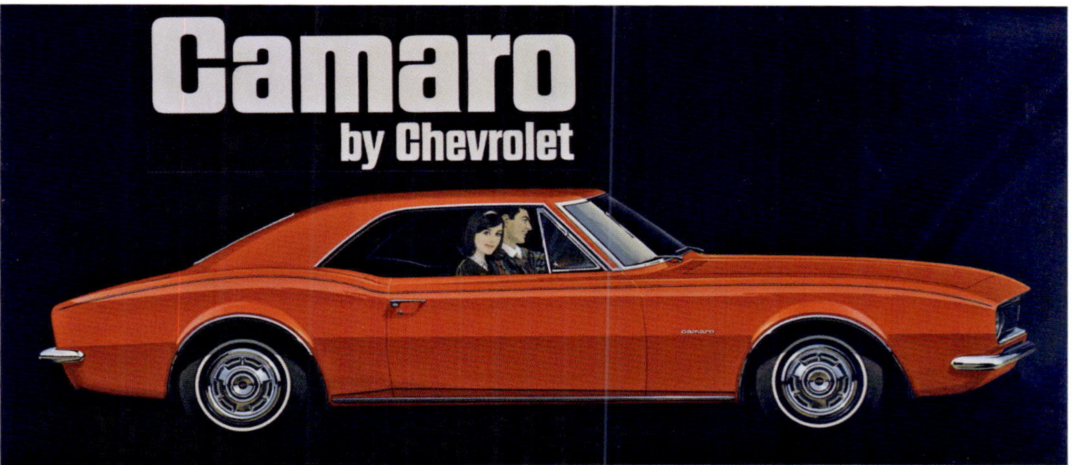

SS

Above: The tidy and sporty interior of the 1967 Camaro.

Left and facing page: Two 1967 Camaros, in base (blue) and SS (yellow) trim.

Above: A promotional photo "exploded" a 1967 Camaro to illustrate its unique, yet simplified, construction.

Right: The Camaro has always stood ready for competition, never put more succinctly than in this 1969 advertisement.

And what does Camaro mean? At the time of the announcement in 1966, the media wondered as well, and they were told that the name was found in an old French-English dictionary, a word of Spanish origin that means "comrade" or "friend." Whether that is true or not, Camaro was not just a good name, it proved to be the perfect name for Chevrolet's new sporty offering.

The name Camaro brought with it no preconceived imagery. It rolled easily off the tongue. It sounded sporty. Exotic.

During the press conference, Estes said that Camaro was a continuation of the sporting character created by the Corvette more than a decade earlier. Not once did he mention the word Mustang. But he didn't have to. Everyone in attendance in Detroit, and those around the country listening by phone, understood the

A word or two to the competition:

You lose.

Camaro SS Sport Coupe with Rally Sport equipment.

Camaro beats all other sporty cars in 1969 Car and Driver Readers' Choice.

Camaro did it. Beat the toughest competition the other cars could muster.

In the kind of contest that really counts.

Every year, *Car and Driver* magazine asks its readers (over half a million at last count) to rate cars. And there's no tougher panel of judges than these real enthusiasts.

Why does the Hugger make it so big with the guys who really know cars? Maybe it's Camaro's looks. Maybe it's Camaro's engines—up to a 396 V8. Maybe it's performance packages, like the eye-popping Z/28. All we know is the competition wasn't in the same ball park. *Car and Driver* readers know, too.

CHEVROLET

Putting you first, keeps us first.

Above: A "cutaway" view of the 1967 Camaro SS model, illustrating its segment-leading packaging characteristics.

Below: A Camaro SS, in red convertible trim. It couldn't get much better than this in 1967.

Above: A 1968 Camaro Z28. Camaros in 1968 differed from 1967 models most notably by the deletion of the side vent window and the addition of side marker lights front and rear.

Below: In 1969, Chevrolet was still touting the Camaro's unique front sub-frame/rear unibody construction at trade and auto shows.

Above: A 1969 Camaro Z28. Fender flares above the wheel wells identify '69 models.

importance of this car in the marketplace and the daunting task that lie ahead for it.

Just a few months later, on September 12, 1966, Chevrolet unveiled the Camaro to the press for the first time, as part of a division-wide product introduction event. So as to maintain the interest of the media for the other products in the Chevy stable, and to add to the suspense, the Camaro was saved for last. When the car, a Camaro SS convertible, was finally revealed, everyone in attendance was in awe. The design was not at all Mustang-like (even though some in Dearborn claimed that it was). The Camaro was more curvaceous, sexier, with what is now referred to as a Coke-bottle shape, particularly when viewed from above.

For the 1967 model year, the Ford Mustang offered five engines of three different displacements, a 200-cubic-inch straight six that produced 120 horsepower, a 289-cubic-inch V8 with horsepower ratings of 200, 225 and 271, and a big-block 390-cubic-inch engine that produced 320 horsepower. The Camaro engines stacked

Above: The Camaro served as the Indianapolis 500 Pace Car in 1969, the second time the Camaro had done so, after performing that duty in its inaugural year in 1967. Camaros would pace the Indy 500 again in 1982, 1993 and 2009.

Right: A 1969 Camaro RS.

California Camaro dreamin'! -- a gorgeous 1969 Z28.

up favorably against the Ford motors, top to bottom, initially offering engines ranging from a 140 horsepower, 230-cubic-inch motor to a 295 horsepower, 350-cubic-inch V8. Bigger motors would soon follow.

Perhaps no better description, or "Camaro philosophy," has been written, then or since, than what appeared in the *Chevrolet Passenger Car Engineering Features* book intended for the media upon the introduction of the Camaro in 1967:

"The sports-like Camaro is an all-new personal car designed to meet the growing American preference for individualized transportation. It is for the driver who likes to drive; the mobility conscious customer who requires a high degree of handling and roadability with a firm, yet comfortable ride; the owner who expects his personal tastes and action to be reflected in a clean, modern, and dynamic styling line and quick, sharply defined performance."

To many Mustang and Camaro aficionados respectively, the 1967 model year offerings remain all-time favorite designs. With the Mustang clearly in the cross-hairs initially, the development team at GM and Chevrolet had succeeded by every measure. The first-generation Camaro was visually stunning and offered more power-train options than the competition. The Camaro forced consumers to finally choose sides. From the late '60s forward, you were either a Camaro fan or a Mustang fan. Given the Herculean challenge, Chevrolet not only hit a home run with the Camaro, it hit a grand slam.

The American muscle-car wars had officially begun.

SUNOCO CAMARO
6
ROGER PENSKE

CHAPTER THREE: **RACING CAMAROS**

"In the late '60s, we considered the Camaro a poor-man's Corvette, and wanted to take it racing. But we had to be careful not to intrude on the Corvette space."

Ernie Callard, retired GM Performance Parts Manager

During most of the '60s, even though General Motors was officially out of racing, a few independent-minded executives at Chevrolet saw the value of supporting, in a back-door way, the NHRA and the newly formed SCCA Trans Am racing series by providing legitimate teams run by Bill "Grumpy" Jenkins and Roger Penske respectively, with performance parts. Retired GM Parts Manager Ernie Callard, then still only in his twenties, made sure teams had access to parts and engines, even if GM was supposed to be looking the other way.

Facing page: The 1969 Sunoco Camaro driven by Mark Donahue (here a restored version) is perhaps the most famous and successful racing Camaro of all time.

Above: A 1967 Camaro paces an SCCA Trans Am race.

Left: Jack Baldwin drives the Hot Wheels Camaro in a 1994 Trans Am contest.

Above: The man within Chevrolet who made sure that race teams had a sufficient supply of parts was Vince Piggins. Piggins also played a key role getting late-'60s COPO Camaros in the hands of dealers.

Above right: Since 1967, Camaros have been common sights at NHRA sanctioned events. This 1968 car was piloted by Hall of Fame driver Bill "Grumpy" Jenkins.

Recalls Callard, "Racers needed parts, so we made sure that a certain number of performance parts were always readily available to dealers upon special request by race teams. Crate motors, sure, but also components like springs, steering gears, stabilizer bars and rear-end assemblies with disc brakes. We had over three hundred part numbers. Even though the teams would have to order the parts through a Chevy dealer, we would often ship parts directly to the team, either at the garage or the track. We maintained a list of preferred racing customers, and our Chevy dealers knew who they were, so dealers were an important part of the process of getting parts to teams quickly."

The driving force for Chevrolet Performance in the '60s was Product Promotions Manager Vince Piggins.

Retired Development Engineer Bill Howell, who worked for Piggins, remembers. "Vince was not particularly high ranking in the big scheme of things at GM, but he had a way of doing what he wanted. He definitely was opinionated. I wouldn't call him arrogant, but he was stand-offish. He was not someone who you could easily get acquainted with. But if you had talent, particularly a talent that he could use, he was very approachable. I guess I had a talent he needed."

Piggins also had plans for the Camaro.

"In the late '60s, we considered the Camaro a poor-man's Corvette," says Callard, "and wanted to take it racing. But we had to be careful not to intrude on the Corvette space."

Howell agrees. "Zora [Arkus-Duntov, Corvette chief engineer] was very protective of the Corvette image. The Trans Am Series was the ideal solution."

Above: A rendering of a Trans Am concept intended to compete in the 1967 series. This sketch was done well before the final Camaro exterior design was approved.

Below: The real 1967 Sunoco Trans Am race car, driven famously by Mark Donahue for Penske-Hilton Racing.

TRANS AM SERIES

In 1966, the Sports Car Club of America (SCCA) launched the Trans Am Series, and it immediately captured the fascination of American race fans. The series initially had two classes: under 2.0 liters and over 2.0 liters. While the lower displacement class featured primarily foreign makes from England and Italy, it was the larger displacement class that made the headlines.

Ford Mustangs not only won races, they began to define the Trans Am "look." And Chevy was on the outside looking in, until 1967.

Coinciding with the launch of the new Camaro that same year, Chevy now had a car to enter, and contracted with Penske-Hilton Racing and driver Mark Donahue to lead the way. Despite three wins, with very little development time, the 1967 season was mostly spent fine-tuning the Camaro Trans Am package. The problems centered primarily around handling and braking.

"The brakes were a disaster," recalls Howell, "and no one knew how to set up the suspension. Donahue and Penske worked hard that first year trying to get things right, and often we didn't have the parts that were required. It was mostly trial and error."

But by the 1968 campaign, Chevy and Penske got it right, and Donahue was clearly the man to beat, winning ten of 13 races, ultimately winning the championship with Camaro that year.

In 1969, Chevrolet, Penske and Donahue repeated their winning ways, and the Camaro was now the hottest car on the track, which, of course, translated to sales on Main Street.

Success breeds success – and expense – and in 1970, Penske and Donahue were wooed by American Motors to campaign its Javelin, winning the championship in 1971. Says Howell, laughing, "Vince used to say that every time Penske would win, the price would go up!

These pages: This car was actually car no. 1 of the 69 COPO ZL1 Camaros built in 1969. It was purchased by Illinois dealer Fred Gibb and modified and driven by Dick Harrell. This car competed in the AHRA series and was AHRA Champion in 1971. The engine, while modified, kept the original aluminum 427 block.

But at the time we just couldn't match the deal made by American Motors. Also, Chevy had just struck a deal with McLaren to do the Can Am series, and maybe Penske wanted a piece of that, too. But the reality was that the only team we had worked with up to that point was Penske, so we felt somewhat at a loss."

Jim Hall and his Chaparral race team replaced Penske in 1970. Just to keep things interesting and competitive, the Ford Mustang, driven by Parnelli Jones, won it all in 1970.

The legendary Smokey Yunick also attempted to enter a Camaro in Trans Am, but his efforts became more infamous than famous, due to his unauthorized modifications. "Smokey and Vince were friends starting with NASCAR," remembers Howell. "But the SCCA wouldn't allow Yunick's Camaro to race because of the modifications. He shaved weight, changed suspension components, control arms, front knuckles, you name it. It seemed that Smokey would rather ask for forgiveness

Perhaps the closest thing to an automotive all-star game was the IROC series. Here, Al Unser Jr. leads Darrell Waltrip and Al Unser Sr. around a turn during a 1986 race. Fans could cheer for their favorite drivers, but no matter who won, a Camaro was always in the Winner's Circle.

than permission." Nevertheless, his brief participation, if nothing else, added to the Camaro lore.

Penske, a long-time Chevrolet dealer, would work with Chevy Performance in the years to come, notably in NASCAR and Indy Car, but the three seasons he successfully campaigned the Trans Am Camaro clearly helped define the lasting, sporting character of Chevrolet's iconic muscle car.

INTERNATIONAL RACE OF CHAMPIONS

The International Race of Champions, or IROC, was simply a stroke of marketing genius: invite the world's top drivers, from both open- and closed-wheel series, put them in the seats of identically prepared cars, and let them battle it out on television in front of millions of viewers.

IROC completed its first season in 1974, using identical Porsche Carrera RSR race cars, with Mark Donahue winning the inaugural season. The next year, Chevrolet took over the IROC sponsorship, and placed some of the world's top drivers in Camaros.

To raise awareness, Chevrolet began running magazine advertisements with the headline, "Gentlemen, start your Camaros." In the accompanying photo, standing behind the no. 12 Camaro of Benny Parsons were Parsons,

Above: Chevrolet touted its International Race of Champions sponsorship with this advertisement that said, simply, "Gentlemen, start your Camaros."

Below: The 1999 edition of Whit Bazemore's Camaro Funny Car.

Even when standing still, IROC Camaro racing machines attract attention.

Brian Redman, James Hunt, Emerson Fittipaldi, Richard Petty, Jody Scheckter, A.J. Foyt, Mario Andretti, Bobby Allison, Al Unser, and David Pearson. Even today, those names ring like a "who's who" of motorsports heroes.

Chevrolet sponsored the IROC Series from 1975 through 1989 (the series was idle from 1981-1983). Bobby Unser won in 1975, the first season under Chevrolet's sponsorship. Foyt won the next two years, followed by Al Unser, Andretti, Allison, Cale Yarborough, Harry Gant, Al Unser Jr., Geoff Bodine and Terry Labonte.

The IROC Series was probably the closest the world of motorsports got to an inter-league all-star game. And every race, every year, there was a Camaro in the winner's circle.

DRAG RACING

From its inception in 1967, the Chevrolet Camaro has been a constant competitor at NHRA events, in both

the sportsman and professional classes. Be it Super Street, Stock, Super Stock, Pro Stock or Funny Car, Camaro has been the vehicle of choice for many drag racers, for many years.

Not the least of whom was career Chevy racer "Grumpy" Jenkins. First with the Chevy II Nova, then the Camaro, and later the lighter-weight Vega, Jenkins was a pioneer in Super Stock and Pro Stock racing. He participated in the Pro Stock class when NHRA launched it in 1970, winning the first two events of the year, the Winternationals and Gatornationals, in a 1968 Camaro.

"We have a long record of competing in NHRA," says Mark Kent, director of racing at GM. "In the amateur classes, lots of people run our cars, but traditionally have done it with limited assistance from us. That's why the COPO Camaro is so important. COPO is a great way to get a more relevant product in the hands of amateur racers."

Kent oversees all on-track elements for GM motorsports activities, including NHRA. In short, he's responsible for having products that can win races. "We need to supply parts in order for these racers to be competitive."

Kent adds, "Getting the COPO Camaro on the track in front of fans will build interest among racers. It will fuel the desire for them to either buy a COPO Camaro, or build their own. The COPO brand provides a great opportunity to sell performance parts."

Ladies and gentlemen, start your Camaros.

For the 2008 SEMA Show, Chevrolet Performance created this show car that paid homage to the iconic #6 Penske-Donahue-Sunoco Trans Am Camaro of 1967 to 1969.

CHAPTER FOUR: **GEN FIVE CAMARO**

"I got goose bumps on my arms when it was announced that the Camaro would return."

Al Oppenheiser, Camaro Chief Engineer

At the conclusion of the 2002 model year, Chevrolet announced that production of the Camaro would end. For Camaro aficionados, the folks at Chevy had done the unthinkable.

The fourth-generation Camaro had aged, and had not been sufficiently updated during its life cycle. Sales had slipped. Furthermore, GM had done little in terms of developing a next-generation Camaro. Rather than keep the aging, uncompetitive Camaro in Chevy showrooms, or try to hastily develop a new car, Chevy pulled the plug.

For 35 years, Camaro had battled head-to-head with the Ford Mustang, and instantly, and so abruptly, Mustang had the segment all to itself. Ford, which had itself fiddled with the Mustang formula in its second generation (the Mustang II from 1974 to 1978) and almost erred again by considering a Mazda-based Mustang in the late '80s (the car that became the Ford Probe), by the new millennium had the Mustang firmly back on track, and in fact was developing its own fifth-generation Mustang for introduction as a 2005 model.

Facing page: A beautiful Camaro RS convertible.

Above: When Camaros are unveiled at auto shows, here a ZL1 Concept, the world's automotive press pay keen attention.

Clay modelers shaping a quarter-scale model of a 5th-generation Camaro.

Despite protests from Camaro owners, in retrospect, Chevy had made the right decision. Step back, take a deep breath, and develop a car once again worthy of the Camaro legacy.

The automotive media almost immediately began to speculate about a new Camaro, despite GM's silence. The Camaro project had two well-placed internal champions however: Bob Lutz, then chairman of GM North America and its well-known "product czar," and Ed Welburn, GM's vice president of design. Having worked at both Ford and Chrysler, Lutz recognized the importance of the Camaro to the Chevy product line-up and to the overall muscle car segment. Welburn understood the role the Camaro could play in establishing a Chevrolet design language.

Lutz and Welburn immediately got Camaro Exterior Designer Tom Peters starting to think in terms of an updated Camaro design. At the 2003 North American International Auto Show in Detroit, Ford tipped its hand by showing its Mustang GT Concept, which strongly hinted at what the 2005 production Mustang would look like. Lutz and Welburn could see that Ford was taking the Mustang back to its roots with a retro-style look reminiscent of the '67 to '69 models. A new Camaro, they surmised, if there was to be one, could draw upon Camaro heritage, but it would have to be a completely modern interpretation.

At the 2004 Detroit Show, Ford unveiled its production Mustang, to be sold as a 2005 model, to universal acclaim. Show goers, still puzzled by Camaro's absence, would have to wait one more year.

On January 6, 2006, literally thousands of journalists and interested industry onlookers jammed into the General Motors display at the North American International Auto Show in Detroit. Auto writers were expecting a Camaro Concept, but had no idea what it would look like.

After a parade of vintage Camaros from each of the four previous generations, the silver Camaro Concept carefully drove out from behind a partition. The concept was slowly driven to a turntable embedded into

Above: The final 2010 Camaro design was kept faithful to this early design sketch.

Below: GM Designer Tom Peters lays tape on a full-scale clay model to indicate the position of the hood.

Above: GM Vice President of Design Ed Welburn reviews a variety of Camaro exterior designs. Welburn insisted that the fifth-generation Camaro be faithful to Camaros of the past, yet not be a "retro" design.

Below: The Camaro Concept was literally swallowed up by the press at its introduction at the 2006 North American International Auto Show in Detroit.

The world's first peek, in 2006, at what would become the fifth-generation Camaro.

the stage floor, and the car did one complete revolution. Automotive journalists, typically somewhat jaded and reserved, could not contain themselves. Amid a multitude of cheers and flashbulbs, the car, driven by Lutz, moved off the stage and parted the crowd on a predetermined path. As the car drove through the press, the ropes were barely enough to contain the crowd. Lutz drove the car to another raised platform and turntable.

The Camaro Concept looked production ready, but to universal dismay, during the press conference, Lutz fell short of confirming that the Camaro would actually be built. That announcement came seven months later on August 10, 2006, when then-Chairman Rick Wagoner uttered his now-famous words, "As evidence that we're not completely brain dead, GM will build the Chevy Camaro."

"The Camaro concept car was unveiled at the 2006 North American International Auto Show in Detroit to gauge the reaction to a new Camaro," says Chief Engineer Oppenheiser. "But we had already begun engineering it as if it was going to be a production vehicle. I got goose bumps on my arms when it was announced that the Camaro would return."

The fifth-generation Camaro was a technological tour de force. It featured an independent rear suspension, a first for Camaro and the "pony car" segment. The new Camaro came with two aluminum-block engines, the 3.6-liter V6 producing 304 horsepower and the 6.2-liter LS3 V8 pumping out a very respectable 426 horsepower (400hp for the automatic transmission-equipped L99 version).

Chevy provided from the factory the kind of oversized wheels that buyers were demanding from the aftermarket, an 18-inch standard wheel (the base wheel on the Mustang was 17 inches), with an optional 19-inch aluminum wheel. The Camaro SS came fitted with huge 20-inch wheels, one of the first production passenger cars to carry wheels so large. In addition, optional 21-inch wheels were available as a Chevrolet accessory. Behind those big wheels were four-wheel disc brakes, standard. Six forward gears, either manual or automatic, the latter featuring paddle shifters (TAPshift) located on the steering wheel.

Inside and out, the Camaro exhibits a crisp, uncluttered design.

It was also the largest Camaro ever. A wheelbase of 112.3 inches was nearly a foot longer than its predecessor and more than five inches longer than a Mustang (it should be noted however that a 2008 Dodge Challenger tops them both, with a wheelbase of 116.0 inches).

When the new Camaro went on sale in the fall of 2009 as a 2010 model, it immediately drove traffic to Chevy dealerships and began to compete with the Mustang again in the sales war. In fact, Camaro outsold Mustang in 2010 and 2011.

It was 1967 all over again.

The bad-to-the-bone ZL1 is as good as a street-legal Camaro can get.

CAMARO ZL1: COPO FOR THE STREET

In 1969, if you were fortunate enough to get your hands on one of the 69 COPO Camaros with the big 427 aluminum-block motor, it came with the designation ZL1.

In 2012, if you were not fortunate enough to land one of the 69 racing COPO Camaros, the fifth-gen Camaro ZL1 was your best alternative.

The ZL1 is as good as a street-legal Camaro gets. Powered by a 6.2-liter (376 cubic inches) all-aluminum LSA V8 supercharged engine, it produces 580 horsepower, far exceeding the power and handling characteristics of the original ZL1.

Explains Oppenheiser: "The ZL1 was re-engineered by 30 percent, all for improved performance. It has a new front end, oil cooler, transmission cooler, rear differential cooler, and belly pan. The ZL1 has to be unbeatable on the race track or the street."

The Camaro ZL1 features the third generation of

Either in coupe or convertible form, the fifth-generation Camaro has returned the Chevrolet muscle car to design prominence.

With outrageous power, Magnetic Ride Control (MRC) and Performance Traction Management (PTM), the street-legal ZL1 is a force to be reckoned with.

Magnetic Ride Control (MRC) previously seen only on the Corvette. MRC employs valve-less damping and magneto-rheological fluid technology. By controlling the electro-magnetic current, the system varies the suspension firmness to match the road and driving conditions. In other words the ZL1 suspension can be adjusted for street, track or strip.

For specific use on the drag strip or race course, the Camaro ZL1 also features Performance Traction Management (PTM) as standard equipment. First introduced on the Corvette ZR1, PTM integrates magnetic ride, launch, traction and electronic stability controls.

The result is a Camaro that is blazingly fast and can compete with the best of the world's super cars. Says Chevy Performance Director Sandor Piszar, convincingly, "The ZL1 is the ultimate Camaro for the street."

"Period."

TOOLS
CHEVROLET

CHAPTER FIVE: **COPO IS REBORN**

"We had the basic blueprint to be competitive in the sportsman classes of NHRA. We knew what to do; we'd done it before."

Jim Campbell, U.S. VP, Performance Vehicles and Motorsports

In Jim Campbell's office is a small "white board" on which is written in dry-erase ink the game plan for the Performance Vehicles and Motorsports team. The diagram is simple, and at first glance not particularly noteworthy - except that the board hasn't been erased in several years. "It's there as a daily reminder for me and the team," he says.

Campbell is Vice President of Performance Vehicles and Motorsports at General Motors. What makes the white board significant is that the 2012 COPO Camaro most likely would not have happened without what is written on it.

Across the top of the board are three boxes. In the first box is written "Performance Variants." In the second box are the words "Performance Parts." And in the third box, "Motorsports, Technical & Marketing." This is Jim Campbell's world.

"Performance Variants" refers to the corporate activity that transforms standard production vehicles into high-performance machines. For Camaro, think SS, 1LE and ZL1. For Cadillac, think V-Series. "Performance Parts" refers to the long-established parts group that supplies crate motors, transmissions, engine components like pistons, cylinder heads and manifolds, electrical and ignition systems, wheels and restoration parts that professionals and amateurs alike can tap into to turn their GM vehicles into high performance screamers. And "Motorsports, Technical & Marketing" refers to, well, motorsports, technical and marketing.

None of this seems particularly groundbreaking, until one realizes that before Jim Campbell came along, the three "boxes" were separate entities within GM, working separately and independently. For the COPO Camaro to happen, the structural and managerial synergy had to be in place. The three "boxes" had to work together.

Explains Sandor Piszar, director of performance vehicles and motorsports, "The departments historically worked separately. The performance group, the parts group and the marketing group were all working independently. COPO would not exist today if we were still operating under the prior system. COPO cuts across all three."

The COPO Camaro story, however, begins at least a half-decade earlier. There were various people and departments working to bring Chevrolet back into NHRA sportsman-class racing.

"We had been working on what was to become the COPO Camaro for many years," explains Mark Kent, Chevrolet's director of racing. "We have a long history of competing in, and supporting, Pro Stock, but it was in the amateur classes that there was a void. Sure, people were racing our products, but they were doing it mostly by themselves."

Around 2006, at the time of the unveiling of the fifth-generation Camaro Concept at the North American

Facing page: A COPO Camaro competing at sportsman class NHRA events was the vision the Chevy Performance Team held from the beginning of the program.

The three available COPO engines were all tested exhaustively in the proof-of-concept car. This is the 327-cubic-inch motor with the 2.9-liter supercharger.

International Auto Show in Detroit, the racing, engineering and marketing groups began working on the idea of a grassroots, factory built racer that would make it easier for racers to compete at the entry levels of NHRA drag racing.

But when GM entered its much-publicized corporate restructuring in 2008, the project came to a screeching halt. "Motorsports was one of the first things to get put on hold," remembers Kent. "Much of the work had been done. We had 'blueprints,' but we had to roll them up and put them away."

"When discussions took place about the possibility of building an NHRA purpose-built Camaro race car, we started to put a profile together of what the car would look like, what engine we might use," remembers Cohen. "We also started to talk about things like logistics, how we could get bodies, motors and components in one place and how and where we might build it. We also started to give thought about costs. We had already done a lot of work."

Two years later, in 2010, the NHRA Camaro project

got jump-started just as the new production Camaros were hitting dealer showrooms in volume.

"In 2010, we were aware of what Ford was doing since 2008 in grassroots racing with its Mustang Cobra Jets," explains Kent. "Even Dodge was getting in on it with its Drag Pak Challengers. It was pretty clear to us that we had to restart our program. So, when we came out of the restructuring, all we had to do was unroll the prints and pick up where we left off." This explains the apparent speed developing the new COPO, because much of the upfront work had already been done.

Adds Campbell, "We had the basic blueprint to compete in the sportsman classes of NHRA. We knew what to do; we'd done it before. The pillars had been in place for many years and we have so many people within the company who are passionate about drag racing. When we re-opened the project we had to verify that our blueprint was still valid. It was."

Still, the project needed approval from GM senior management to proceed.

Campbell set up separate meetings with Mark Reuss, GM president of North America, and Tom Stephens, GM vice chairman and chief technology officer, to gauge their interest and, hopefully, approve expenditures. To prepare for the meetings, Campbell and his team armed themselves with data and even sketches of what the car might look like.

Stephens, a former drag racer, and Reuss were equally passionate about the COPO Camaro proposal. They agreed that the project had to support itself.

Campbell proposed building one car, a "proof-of-concept" vehicle, to test the waters. And the perfect place to gauge reaction would be at the annual SEMA (Specialty Equipment Market Association) Show in Las Vegas later that year. Stephens and Reuss agreed, and gave Campbell the green light to proceed with the proof-of-concept car. It was also decided that this project, if successful, would be worth carrying the revered "COPO" name. Fortunately the team had the foresight to trademark the COPO name in 2006. Though called a proof-of-concept, it was to be anything but a concept car. This was to be a real "runner" and, in fact, would carry serial no. 1 if any future COPO Camaros were to be built.

Campbell then assigned Mark Kent the responsibility to build the proof-of-concept vehicle in time for SEMA.

That was the good news. The bad news was that there were only ten months until the SEMA Show in November. There was no time to lose. Kent quickly pulled his team together.

Fortunately, a lot of the groundwork had been done.

"The various groups were already working on performance ideas, so when Jim Campbell said, 'Let's do this,' we could immediately pull studies out of our pockets," says Oppenheiser. "We definitely had a head start."

PROOF-OF-CONCEPT WORK BEGINS

One of the persons Kent contacted first was Russ O'Blenes, manager of racing powertrains and advanced projects, who had been directly involved in racing for more than 20 years, has a no-nonsense demeanor, and a track record for getting things done. He oversees the engineering of racing engines and performance crate motors for Chevrolet. It's an area of the company where there is little, if any, margin for error. Performance engines are hand-built at this small, yet very high-tech facility in a quiet industrial park in Wixom, Michigan, northwest of Detroit.

O'Blenes, in turn, tapped Robin Wright to be project manager.

Wright was the ideal choice. For starters, he had long been involved in drag racing at the amateur level. Secondly, Wright had already done a feasibility study at O'Blenes' request thatplayed a key role in gaining approval for the project.

Wright's initial responsibilities were to generate a bill of materials. In other words, what components and parts were necessary to build the proof-of-concept vehicle.

He had to create a statement of work, all of the specifications and the technical aspects of the vehicle. He had to engage suppliers and source component hardware.

Visitor
Information
ENCE

"Performance is a part of our DNA, It's part of our history and heritage."

And finally, he had to select and test concept powertrains and, as part of O'Blenes' team, he was in precisely the right location.

The next major issue to resolve was how, but more importantly, who, was to build the proof-of-concept vehicle. Building a drag car requires very specialized knowledge. Moreover, the car had to meet NHRA requirements and certifications right out of the box.

In October of 2010, Kent, O'Blenes and Wright had paid a visit to NHRA headquarters and shared with them their idea to re-enter stock drag racing. "We got a verbal buy-in from NHRA as a result of that meeting," recalls O'Blenes. "That was a big deal; pretty much unprecedented."

The NHRA also recommended several builders, one of whom was Mike Pustelny at MPR Race Cars. Pustelny, a former GM employee himself, was well known to the NHRA. Conversely, Pustelny well understood the NHRA build requirements. Chevrolet and Pustelny would only get one shot at building the proof-of-concept car if the SEMA deadline was to be met.

Oh, yes. Pustelny had also recently completed builds for Mustang Cobra Jet and Challenger Drag Pak race cars, so he understood the competition very well.

"It took five months to build the proof-of-concept vehicle," says O'Blenes. "It was a joint effort between Chevrolet and Mike Pustelny."

At the same time, Pustelny praised his Chevy counterparts, not the least of whom was Wright, who served as his single point of contact at Chevrolet. "It simplified things for me that I only had one primary contact at Chevrolet," remembers Pustelny. "Robin made good decisions, real quick. Most importantly, he never deviated from the plan. Otherwise, it would have been impossible to build this car so quickly."

As components began to arrive at MPR Race Cars, Pustelny began the engineering and build of the proof-of-concept vehicle. Meanwhile, the rest of the team was focused on the launch event.

THE ROAD TO SEMA

In early October 2011, Pustelny was ready to "deliver" the proof-of-concept vehicle to Chevy Performance for sign-off. Campbell, Kent, Piszar and Meyer drove out to Pustelny's shop. O'Blenes and Wright drove separately and had gotten there a little earlier to help Pustelny prepare for the review.

Once everyone was assembled, Pustelny proceeded with the walk-through, going over the proof-of-concept vehicle in painstaking detail, explaining the primary component systems and the various modifications. He also told the team that the car had received either the necessary approvals or tentative approvals from NHRA.

Finally, Pustelny invited Campbell to climb inside. Campbell started the engine, and gave it a few taps of the throttle. The roar inside Pustelny's small shop was deafening. The entire team was grinning. The car had been completed. "It was an unbelievable feeling," recalls Campbell.

About a week later, all of the Chevrolet cars that were intended to be shown at the SEMA Show were assembled at the GM Heritage Center for a review by GM management and company insiders. The bevy of amazing Camaro show cars heading to Las Vegas

Facing page: At its unveiling at the SEMA Show, the COPO proof-of-concept was the center of attention.

The proof-of concept car getting a performance shake-down at Bradenton Motorsports Park.

included the Camaro Red Zone Concept, the Camaro Synergy Series Concept, the Camaro 1LE Concept, the Camaro ZL1 Carbon Concept, and the Hot Wheels™ Concept. But none garnered as much attention as the highly-anticipated COPO Camaro Concept.

Campbell remembers. "We did a COPO walk-through for Tom Stephens. After a pause, Tom says, 'Can you fire this thing up?' and we did! It was very loud, of course, but the positive reaction from the people in attendance was incredible."

Adds Wright, "The internal audience reaction was remarkable and, we hoped, indicative of what the public reaction would be at SEMA."

On Monday, October 31, 2011, the day before the official opening of the SEMA Show, the automotive press and interested onlookers gathered in the Gold Lot of the Las Vegas Convention Center for the COPO Camaro unveiling. The only thing visible, however, was an oversized wooden crate. Affixed to the sides of this crate were four signs with this simple inscription:

"Performance is a part of our DNA," Campbell told the crowd. "It's part of our history and heritage. We're here at SEMA. It's all about performance enhancements and we're ready to introduce the COPO Camaro Concept. Fire it up!"

At that, Pustelny started the ignition and punched the throttle to the absolute delight of the crowd and drove the COPO Camaro out of the makeshift box..

The inscription on the crate, P/N 20129562, referred

to the single Chevy Performance part number it would take to order the car. The first four digits refer to the year, the last four digits is the next sequence to the two famous COPO order numbers from 1969, no. 9560 (aluminum-block ZL1) and no. 9561 (iron-block L72).

A few months before the SEMA roll-out, Piszar, Cohen and Performance Marketing Manager Jamie Meyer met to discuss the part number that would be assigned to the COPO Camaro if it were to be built. The COPO Camaro would carry a Chevrolet Performance part number and would be ordered as such. "We understood the incredible heritage," explains Piszar, "so this part number would be a continuation of the COPO legacy."

Over the next four days of the SEMA Show, the Chevy Performance team was on hand to field questions, but more importantly, to gauge reaction to the car. Once the car was on the show floor in the Chevy display, it was a human magnet. "We had to pull people off the car," laughs Piszar.

Chevy Performance Assistant Program Manager Steve Johnson explains, "At the SEMA Show, we distributed business reply cards that asked attendees not only if they were interested in the COPO Camaro, but would they purchase one if given the opportunity. In total we received 3,200 response cards. To be honest, we were amazed by the overwhelming response, but

The COPO proof-of-concept car is unveiled at the 2011 SEMA Show in Las Vegas. The number 20129562 is the continuation of the COPO number assigned to ZL1 Camaros in 1969.

it certainly confirmed the interest in the COPO Camaro."

These responses, as well as those collected at the Performance Racing Industry show, the Scottsdale Barrett-Jackson auction and NHRA races, were a critical component of reinstating the Central Office Production Order process.

"The COPO Camaro was a huge hit at the SEMA show, and was the turning point for gauging the interest in building a limited run of COPO production cars," says Marketing Manager Cohen. "One visitor came up to me and said, 'There are two things I have, money and time, but I don't know how much I have of the latter. I want this car now!'"

PERFORMANCE CONFIRMATION

From Las Vegas, the proof-of-concept car was loaded on a transport truck and moved to Orlando, Florida, for the Performance Racing Industry Trade Show, December 1-3, 2011. Again the reaction, this time from the racing community, was very positive.

From Orlando, the proof-of-concept was trucked the 100 miles or so to Bradenton, Florida, and the Bradenton Motorsports Park, where the car would get its first serious performance shake-down on December 5. The car made ten runs on the drag strip, first with the 2.9-liter supercharged 327, and then the naturally aspirated the 427 LS engine. Mike Pustelny was behind

the wheel. "The car was extremely smooth," he remembers. "It handled real well and gave no false signals."

"The car was prepped perfectly and ran great all day," recalls O'Blenes. "This was mainly a shake down and to make sure we were where we needed to be from a competitive standpoint."

Adds Cohen, "To be able to get out and finally have the vehicle go down the track and to see some of the numbers it turned in, was something really exciting to see. I'm proud to say that the vehicle had met or exceeded every expectation we had for it. The vehicle went down the track and turned the times we thought it would. We left the track that day very, very satisfied."

"It's no secret that we got started late in NHRA Stock competition relative to Ford and Dodge," says O'Blenes. "People won't remember their first attempts a few years ago, but they will see our first attempt. In other words, we will be compared to mature products. We had to be competitive right from the start, and we were."

With confirmed customer interest, and performance confirmation, only one thing remained: corporate approval to build more. In mid-December, 2011, Mark Reuss made the call to Jim Campbell's office.

The COPO Camaro project had gotten the green light.

Hoosier
Hoosier

CHAPTER SIX: **PROOF-OF-CONCEPT**

"The COPO name carries with it a tremendous amount of history. The pride and the ambition that everyone related to this project has poured into it to make it successful is just amazing. It can't fail and it won't fail."

Mike Pustelny, MPR Race Cars

Mike Pustelny, owner of MPR Race Cars, will never forget the day he got the early January 2011 call. Out of just a few potential builders, he was the one selected to help build the COPO Camaro proof-of-concept vehicle. It probably shouldn't have come as a big surprise, though.

First of all, he and Project Manager Robin Wright had met each other some years before through drag racing. Moreover, Pustelny was on the short list of builders suggested by the NHRA. If the proof-of-concept car was to be built on time, the builder would need to keep the NHRA in the loop every step of the way so the car could pass technical inspections as the car was being built.

There were two more good reasons Pustelny was selected: first, he was geographically close to GM operations in metropolitan Detroit, and second, he already had built Ford Mustang Cobra Jet and Dodge Challenger Drag Pak racers, so he knew the competitive landscape.

In years past, the relationship between Pustelny and the NHRA technical department might have been described, politely, as tense. But over the years, the relationship grew to one of mutual respect – and trust. "I like to think we both mellowed a bit," laughs Pustelny. Mellowed or not, it was a relationship born out of necessity, and during the Camaro proof-of-concept build, Pustelny would send photos to the NHRA technical staff every few days.

This would not be like other builds, however. For existing race cars, like the Cobra Jet, which debuted in 2008 or the Drag Pak, which debuted in 2010, dimensions had already been established, parts were already specified and approved, and templates were made. But the COPO proof-of-concept project was a clean-sheet approach and Pustelny would need to work closely with the Chevrolet Performance team every step of the way.

Chevy Performance provided most of the specifi-

Facing page: The COPO proof-of-concept, at the time of its completion in October of 2011, before the addition of its graphics.

Above: The first challenge of the proof-of-concept build was to determine ride height and suspension geometry, from which all other measurements would be based.

Above: The proof-of-concept car, still wearing its original yellow paint, with the black front and rear fascias from the "donor" car.

Below: COPO Project Manager Robin Wright, left, looking over dynamometer results.

Left: Prior to welding, the bar stock was placed inside the car to ensure proper roll-cage fit.

Below: The front roll cage is fitted so as to ensure the proper installation of the instrument panel and windshield.

cations. The NHRA mandated others. Still others were unknown, and Pustelny would either engineer a solution, based on prior knowledge, or simply through trial and error.

Wright had already broken the news that the car would be needed in time for the SEMA Show in Las Vegas in late October 2011. The team knew that in order to get the car done in that time frame, interruptions and red tape would have to be kept to a minimum. Wright served as the single point of contact for Pustelny, and it worked beautifully.

"I know that Robin didn't work alone, that there was a great team at Chevrolet working on this project as well," recalls Pustelny. "But the fact that I only had one contact simplified everything for me. If I needed a part,

Above: Rear suspension geometry prototype.

a component, or a decision, Robin would always come through. Sometimes he surprised me with his skill at getting things done, keeping things moving. Again, I knew he wasn't working alone, but for me, he was the face of Chevy Performance."

COPO DESIGN

A car as iconic as the COPO Camaro had to have the right look, a look both classic and contemporary. Dave Ross understands this.

Ross, design manager for Chevrolet Performance and Racing, was given the responsibility of giving the COPO Camaro its memorable look.

"I've been a part of the current COPO project from the very beginning," Ross says. "Even before the fifth-generation Camaro hit the streets, I got a call from [GM Vice President of Design] Ed Welburn to start putting some sketches together."

Welburn was a good friend of hall-of-fame drag racer Bill "Grumpy" Jenkins, as they had both grown up in the Philadelphia area, and in 2008 he planned a meeting with Jenkins to share some ideas.

Chevrolet had been talking about reviving a factory-built Stock Eliminator Camaro, a successor to the legendary special-order cars of 1969. To prepare for the private meeting, Welburn asked Ross to prepare design illustrations of what the car might look like.

As a lifelong enthusiast and former Stock Eliminator racer, Ross was the perfect choice. "A race car is incredibly constrained from a design point of view. It's all about performance," explains Ross. "It's really that simple. We try to take the weight out, reducing everything to the bare essentials. As such, design needs to be both limited and selective."

That initial meeting between Jenkins and Welburn spawned the next step a few years later: preparing a COPO design concept for the 2011 SEMA Show. For this first car, Ross chose the color white for the body, accented with a blue "hockey stick" body stripe.

"Racing design is purely philosophical," explains Ross. "The purpose, after all, is to go fast. Very few cars in the world go fast and look good."

Sandor Piszar, director of Chevy Performance, adds, "We intentionally kept the look low key. We wanted to be faithful to the original COPO Camaro, the one with the 'dog-dish' hubcaps. The original COPO Camaro looked like everyone else's Camaro . . . until the light turned green!"

THE BUILD BEGINS

On a gray day in late February 2011, a large semi-trailer lumbered up the gravel road leading to the MPR Race Cars shop in rural Almont, Michigan, a small village about 40 miles north of Detroit. Wright had arranged for a Camaro body-in-white to be delivered to Pustelny's shop. The body-in-white, actually painted yellow, had come from GM's Milford, Michigan, Proving Ground. Immediately, Pustelny knew he had run into his first problem.

Inside the trailer, the body-in-white was secured to a large wooden pallet. The problem? There was no way to get the car out of the trailer. The forklift was not big enough. The driver was instructed to take the body-in-white to a nearby warehouse, where the trailer could be backed up to a raised loading dock. There, the body and pallet were dragged out of the trailer and loaded onto a conventional flat-bed hauler. Once back at the shop the flat-bed was tilted back and the car was gently winched down to the ground. From there, the body-in-white was cut loose from the pallet and eight men carried it directly to the surface plate.

The heavy steel surface plate is absolutely level, so that the team could begin establishing measurements.

The first task was to determine the ride height of the vehicle, from which all subsequent measurements would be based. There were no wheels or tires, mind you, just a body-in-white and four jack stands. This is where Pustelny's racecar-building expertise first came into play.

"I knew I had to get the body as low to the ground as possible, yet not so low as to drag any parts," he explains. "Even though I didn't have parts yet, I had a good idea of how far the headers and the differential would hang below the car. That was my starting point."

Most race car projects start with one car, not two, but

Above left: Additional support structure was welded to the body floor pan, to which the roll cage was attached.

Above right: Alignment and fitment of the roll cage was critical so that the windshield could be installed without obstruction.

Above: The racing seat placed into position to check ergonomics as well as to ensure clearance of the roll cage.

to facilitate a fast build, Chevrolet Performance planned on providing a body-in-white, plus a complete production Camaro, to pull parts from.

One of the benefits of starting with a body-in-white, rather than a complete car, was that valuable time was not spent disassembling the car, piece-by-piece, to get it down to the bare shell. The second car was needed from which to source parts, front and rear fascia assemblies, instrument panel, steering assembly, glass, headliner, etc.

The "donor" car wasn't delivered until May, so the first weeks were spent welding in additional frame members and to measure, fit and weld the roll cage.

The rear axle and suspension also required a creative solution. A drag car requires a solid rear end, yet the fifth-generation Camaro comes from the factory with an independent rear suspension. In such cases, the NHRA specifies that an alternate rear-end design come from the corporate "parts bin." In this case, the "accepted" heavy-duty nine-inch axle is based on a Chevrolet Trail Blazer, even though the new COPO rear end is sourced

from Strange Engineering of Morton Grove, Illinois. The "new" rear end was designed and constructed following guidelines from Chevrolet Performance, the NHRA technical director and Pustelny. Once at least 50 cars are built, the new suspension becomes the default "stock" suspension for the COPO drag cars only.

When the black donor car was delivered in May, a pre-production Camaro SS, the team was ready to begin transferring components to the new car. By the end of June, the rolling chassis was complete, with tentative approval from the NHRA on the rear suspension and the construction details. And when the engine was delivered from Racing Powertrain in August, an aluminum-block, 427-cubic-inch, naturally aspirated, LS7 V8, the car was nearing completion.

The final touch was the one-of-a-kind COPO wheels. Rich Bogart, of Bogart Wheels, was asked to make a 15-inch wheel that would be exclusive to the proof-of-concept, a wheel design based upon the optional wheel for the Camaro ZL1. The resulting wheel was perfect.

Above: Not originally a part of the "body-in-white," this original-equipment structure supports the instrument panel and provides additional strength to the front end.

Above: The proof-of-concept car, having returned from the paint shop and in its final white color, is nearing completion.

Right: The Powerglide transmission, as seen from the underside of the car.

Above: The finished interior, complete with window netting, awaits only the installation of the interior door panels.

The build team had little more than seven months to build a competitive Stock Eliminator drag car from scratch. In reality, it took about five.

In early October 2011, the car was ready to be delivered to Chevrolet at a "sign-off review." Performance Vehicles and Motorsports VP Jim Campbell was there to inspect the car and either accept it or order further work. Also in attendance were other members of the Chevy Performance team: Mark Kent, Sandor Piszar, Russ O'Blenes, Jamie Meyer and Jeff Kettman. Project Manager Robin Wright was there, of course. Wright and Pustelny, while confident in the end result, were still anxious to see how the car would be received. The proof-of-concept Camaro had been their all-consuming project for seven months.

When the group entered the shop, the white proof-

The 4-inch aluminum driveshaft connects to the 9-inch Strange Engineering rear end.

of-concept Camaro was front-and-center. Off to the side, in a corner, was a Ford Cobra Jet Mustang. In the opposite corner, a Dodge Drag Pak Challenger. This was the first time the three factory drag racing efforts would be seen together in the same place at the same time.

The Camaro proof-of-concept car looked good. It looked aggressive by itself, but on the drag strip, the Camaro would soon approach the starting line opposite these other cars and the team wanted Jim Campbell to see how the Camaro would stack up.

But initially, for this meeting, the focus was all on the Camaro.

The review began at the front of the car and covered every detail of everything that had been done to transform a stock Camaro into a Stock Eliminator. Then, the exterior "walk-around" moved to the interior, which was reviewed with the same painstaking detail as the outside.

Then Campbell climbed into the driver's seat. Up until then, the shop had been totally quiet, except for the voices of the reviewers. Campbell was asked if he would like to fire it up and drive it outside.

"The honor of firing it up for the first time ought to

go to the guy who's team funded it," explains Pustelny.

At the front of the headliner, at the top of the windshield, was a bank of toggle switches. The switch at the left turned the system on. The next one to the right was the ignition switch.

Campbell reached up and flipped the system switch. Then, he moved his hand to the next switch.

The proof-of-concept COPO Camaro roared to life.

"It was an amazing moment I'll never forget," remembers Campbell, "marking another key development step to reaching our goal."

Above: A thing of beauty. The finished proof-of-concept car driven out of the MPR Race Car shop for the first time.

Left: The one-of-a-kind serial tag, 2012 COPO POC S/N 001, is perhaps worth its weight in gold, identifying this car as the COPO proof-of-concept car. There will never be another tag like it.

CHAPTER SEVEN: **COPO BUILD**

"The new COPO Camaro is literally the first-ever race car that Chevrolet has developed for consumers to purchase. We had to get it right."

Sandor Piszar, Chevrolet Performance Director

The remaining COPO Camaros would be built exactly like the first proof-of-concept car: Each COPO was crafted one at a time.

It is one thing to build a single race car, but it's quite another to build 68 more with consistent build quality and specifications, all for retail sale.

"Back in 1969," explains Sandor Piszar, Chevrolet Performance Director, "the COPO Camaro was a production vehicle. You could register it, put a plate on it and drive it on the street. The 2012 COPO Camaro is an all-out race car. It doesn't carry a vehicle identification number. Rather, it has a serial number and is actually a Chevy Performance part. It can't be registered for street use. The new COPO Camaro is literally the first-ever race car that Chevrolet has developed for consumers to purchase. We had to get it right. The proof-of-concept provided a solid foundation."

But even as the proof-of-concept car was being built, there was much work to do internally at GM. The most immediate challenge: sourcing Camaro bodies from the factory. On February 2, 2012, Chief Engineer Al Oppenheiser, Piszar, Performance Build Center members Russ O'Blenes and Robin Wright, and Racing Purchasing Manager Jeff Kettman met with the management of GM's Oshawa, Ontario, plant, the sole manufacturing facility

Facing page: A COPO "body-in-white" is masked in preparation for painting, wherein the interior, roll cage and engine bay are painted black.

Above: Another Camaro "body-in-white" masked in preparation for interior painting.

Right: Chevy Performance Director Sandor Piszar, left, and Performance Parts Marketing Manager Cliff Cohen survey a nearly-completed COPO Camaro at the Build Facility.

for Camaros, to determine if, and how, Camaro bodies could be obtained.

To the uninitiated, it might seem easy to get a single body-in-white out of a factory, but for a facility geared for mass production, where timing and sequencing are critical, such is not the case.

The term "body-in-white" refers to an unpainted or "white-steel" body, devoid of any added parts. In the case of GM, it can also mean a steel shell that has been primed and painted, but still without additional parts. In other words, a body-in-white has been stamped, welded and painted, but has not yet entered the vehicle assembly line.

The Oshawa Assembly Plant is one of the most flexible auto plants in the world and often ranks among the highest quality plants in the auto industry. With about 10 million square feet of floor space and almost 6,000 employees, it also ranks as one of the largest.

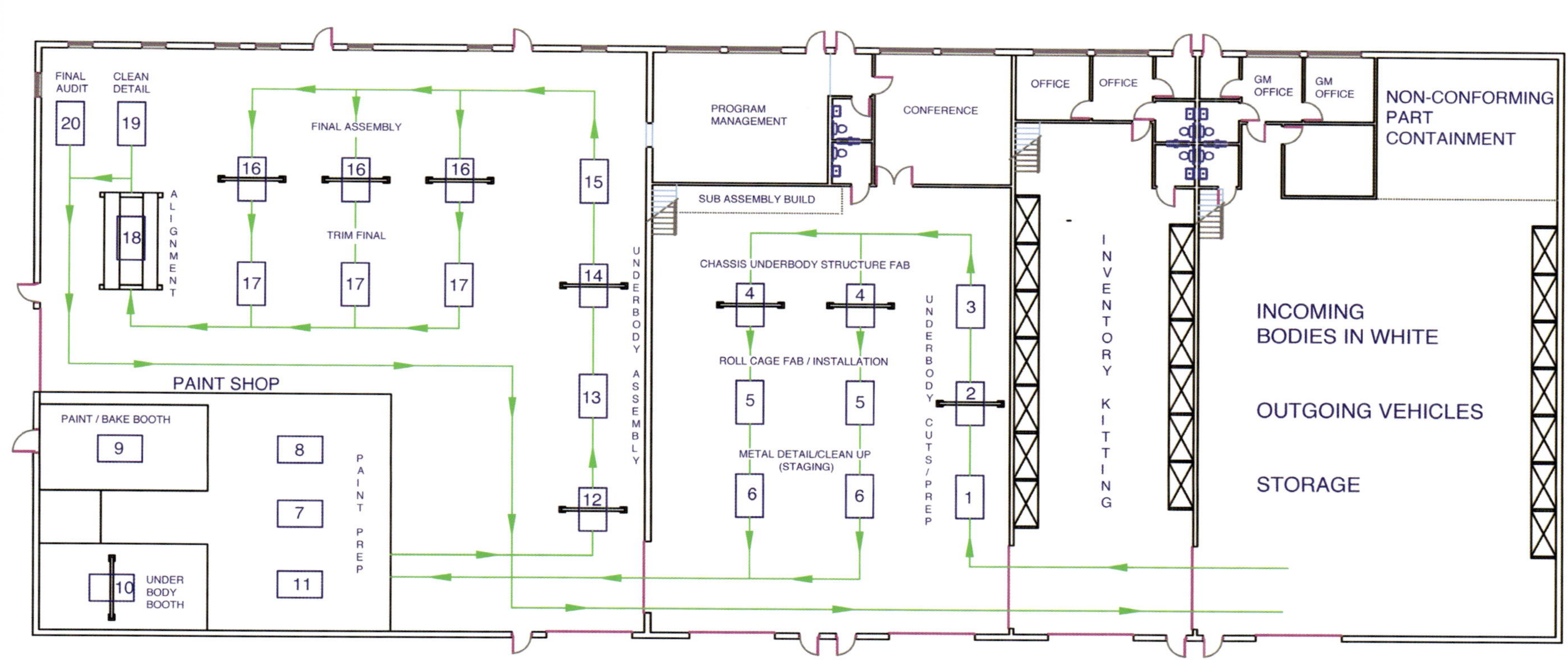

Above: The floor plan of the COPO Build Facility illustrates the smooth flow of fabrication and assembly for the limited-production run of COPO Camaros.

Below: Build Facility managers Roger Allen, left, and Rich Rinke check out the prototype COPO hood, with the COPO and Chevy logos molded in the underside panel.

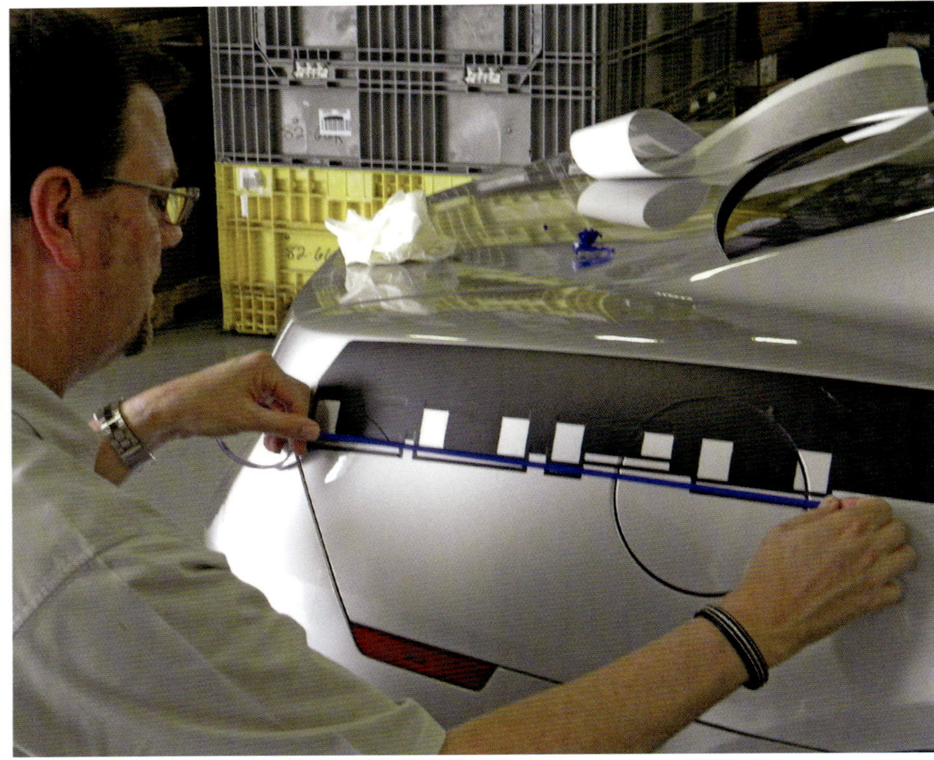

Above left: Unique suspension and brake components are provided by Strange Engineering.

Above right: GM and COPO designer David Ross lays out the unique COPO graphics on a prototype vehicle.

Right: The COPO logo can be seen everywhere, including on this Holley intake manifold for the 427 LS engine.

The COPO team gathered in a conference room at the Oshawa Plant that cold February morning to discuss the COPO project. Representing Oshawa were Plant Manager Daniel Hermer, Assistant Plant Manager Gerald Meek, Contoller Michael Gleeson, Area Plant Manager Paul McLaughlin, Production Paint Coordinator Ronald Gannon, Supply Chain Director Jean Longtin and Material Production and Control Manager Shawn McMahon. This group had support personnel attending as well. The large number of Oshawa representatives and the breadth of their responsibilities attested to the complexity of the request.

"Getting all the necessary parts and components pooled together," explains Wright, "parts that were never intended to be pooled together, and delivered to the right place at the right time, for such few cars, is like going to Venus for the weekend."

The harsh reality was that if for any reason Oshawa could not, or would not, supply Camaro bodies, the COPO project would end just as it was getting started.

Piszar began by outlining the entire COPO plan.

Above: Each assembly station has a simple list of operations to be performed.

As it turned out, it didn't require much convincing to get the Oshawa staff enthusiastic about the project. The Oshawa team just needed to figure out a way to get the bodies built.

Because the COPO Camaros are not production vehicles, they carry no vehicle identification number, or VIN. Rather, they carry serial numbers, simply 1 through 69. Once the colors were determined for each vehicle, the bodies were sequenced as "special build" units. The bodies were stamped, welded, primed, painted and clear-coated. As the COPO units exited the paint area, they were routed off-line so as not to interfere with the sequencing of normal Camaro production vehicles.

"The Oshawa team, led by Hermer, was an invaluable partner in bringing the COPO Camaro to life," explains Piszar. "They were excited about the project

Right: Steel tubing waiting to be transformed into COPO roll cages.

Below left: All of the necessary documentation is kept with the vehicle throughout the build process, much of which is given to the customer upon delivery.

Below right: The COPO logo appears on the throttle body inlet.

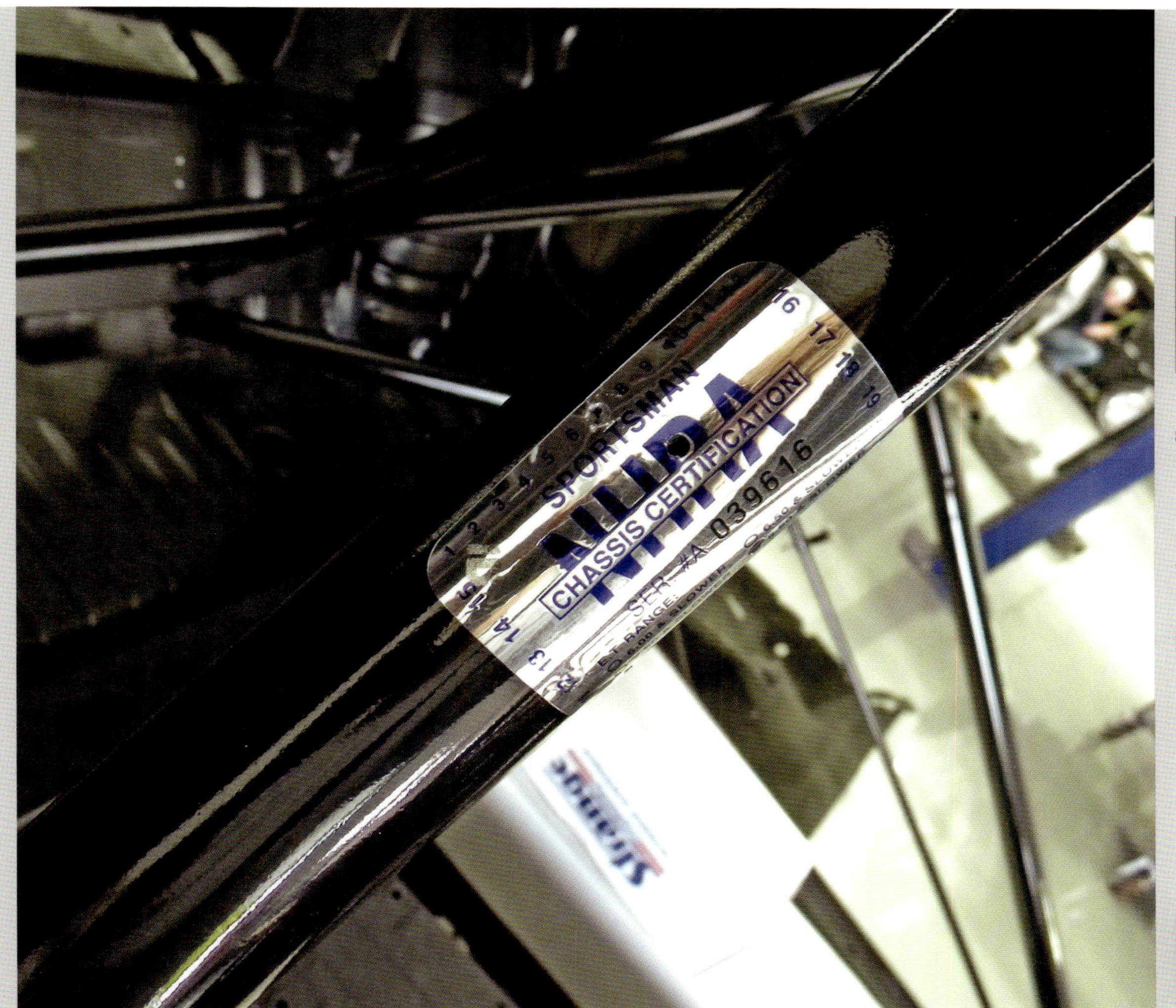

Above left: Each COPO chassis and roll cage is approved and certified by the National Hot Rod Association.

Above right: Experienced craftsmen build each COPO race car by hand.

Left: The engine installed in car serial no. 2, a 327 with a 4.0-liter supercharger, well before trim pieces and front fascia are attached.

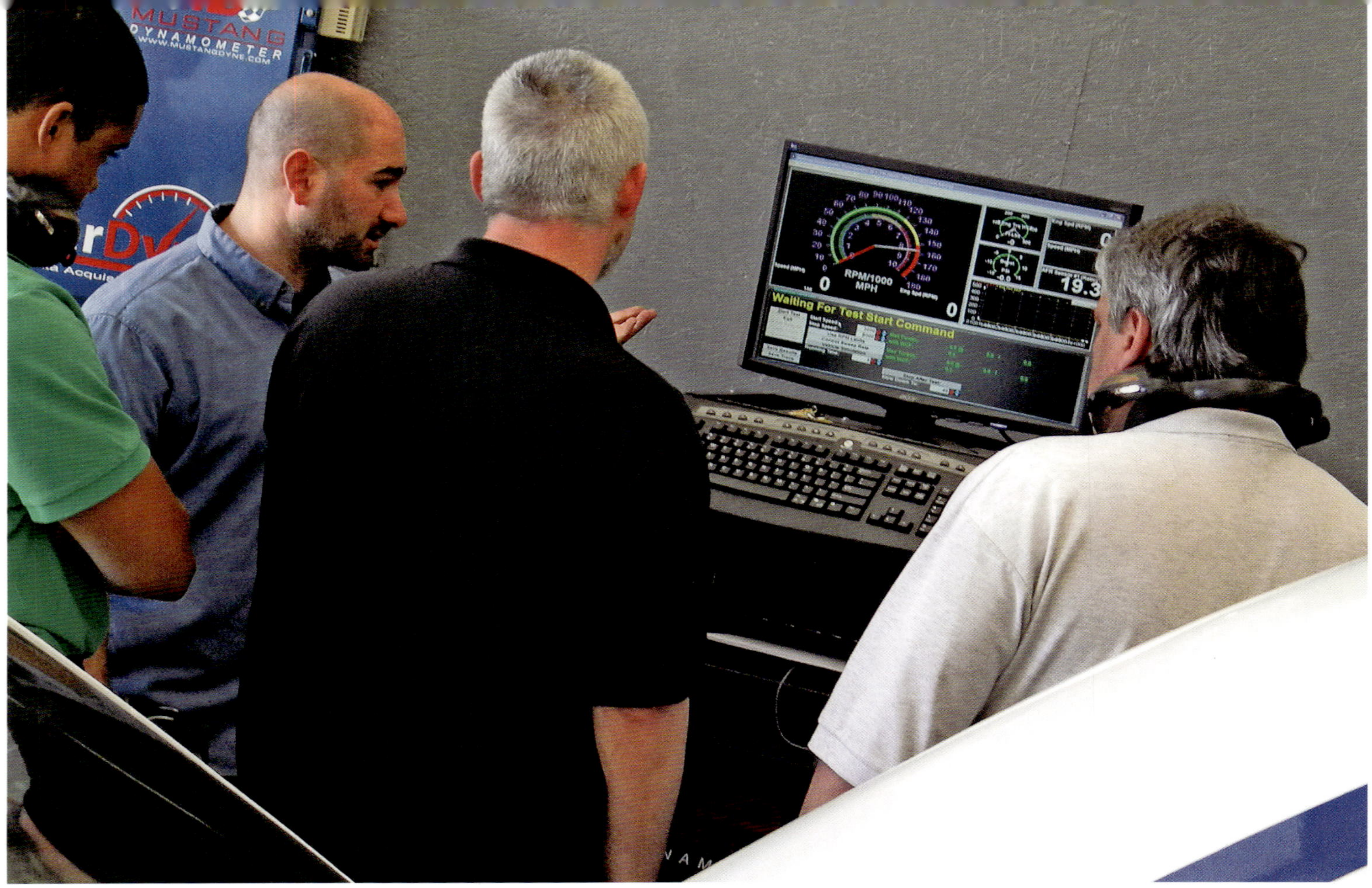

Right: Reviewing engine performance data.

Below: These finished COPO Camaros await only the application of graphics.

and provided extensive support to get the job done. COPO is a small project in the context of running a large production plant, with all the special logistics that it involves. Oshawa took on the extra work to create special processes to build bodies to COPO specifications, pull the required hardware and body components and ship everything to our COPO Build Facility. This extraordinary support shows their strong enthusiasm for what COPO stands for."

The team worked closely with Gannon for the bodies and with McMahon and English for component support. Oppenheiser praises the Oshawa team: "Had it been a different plant, it might have been more difficult. Manufacturing plants by nature don't like to vary from their routines. But the team in Oshawa couldn't have been more accommodating and excited about the project. Oshawa is simply one of the best plants in the world."

Left: The interior of a recently completed COPO Camaro. Only the first few cars received the stainless steel transmission-tunnel cover, before a running change was made to a carpeted tunnel.

Below: Chevy Performance Team members would routinely sign the transmission tunnel before assembly to authenticate the COPO model. Here, team members Roger Allen, Al Oppenheiser and Sandor Piszar added their signatures.

The team also was indebted to Lisa Grassi, product manager for engines & performance at the GM Customer Care & Aftersales (CCA) division (formerly known as Service Parts Operations, which included AC Delco, Divisional and Performance Parts). Grassi was the team's interface for product support from CCA and helped with component coordination between CCA and Oshawa. CCA provided some basic hardware items for COPO assembly, as well as some larger items such as the battery, engine cradle, intercooler pump and steering knuckles.

THE CHEVROLET PERFORMANCE BUILD CENTER

A visit to the Chevrolet Performance Build Center in Wixom, Michigan, is any "gear-head's" dream. The nondescript building in an out-of-the-way industrial park is split into two sections. The section to the north is where high-performance power plants are engineered and developed. The section to the south is where those same engines are hand assembled.

Just as the engine is the heart of an automobile, so too, was the Performance Build Center the heart of the COPO Project. To be sure, the COPO team is spread across many GM facilities, but it was here at the Build Center that the first outline for the resurrected COPO project was undertaken in 2010. It is the home of Russ O'Blenes, manager of GM Racing powertrains, and Robin Wright, COPO project manager. It is the place where COPO owners have the option to build their own engines and where some customers took delivery of their COPO Camaros.

A small sign on the grounds could easily be missed. The best hint of what goes on inside this high-security facility are the pristine semi-trailers belonging to high-profile race teams parked outside.

The Chevrolet Performance Build Center is where General Motors builds only its highest-performance engines and crate motors – and the only place the COPO

Right: The unique convertible body of car no. 69 is the only COPO painted in the Inferno Orange color.

Below: Quality-checking the rear-end and suspension assembly is critical to the COPO Camaro's performance characteristics.

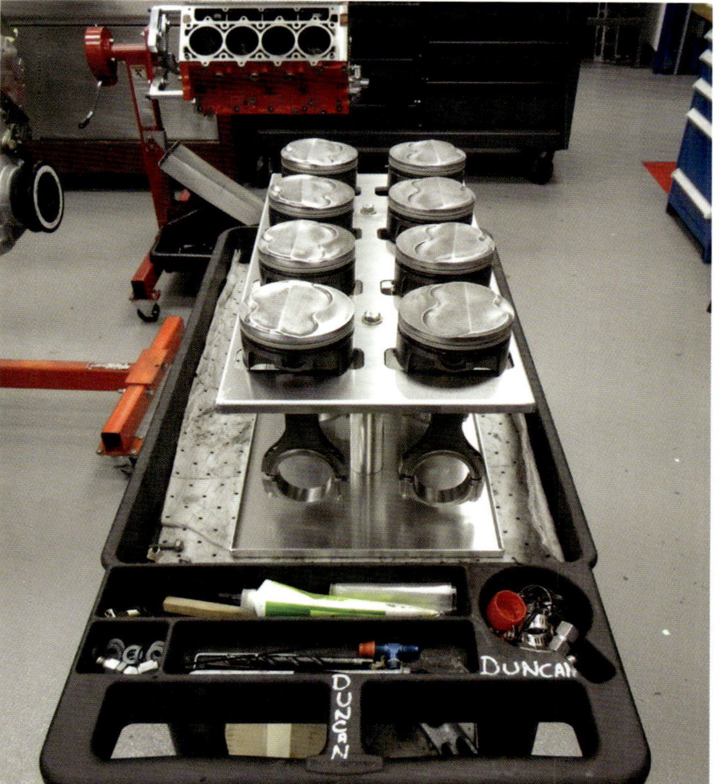

This page: The engine is the heart of any race car, and the 2012 COPO Camaro offers three choices, a 427-cubic-inch naturally aspirated LS and two 327-cubic-inch motors, one with a 2.9-liter supercharger, the other with a 4.0-liter blower.

engines are assembled. The Build Center is known for building the famous LS7 and LS9 engines for the super-high-performance Corvette Z06 and ZR1.

The facility more closely resembles an operating room than an engine assembly plant. The center employs only 14 expert builders, and completes just 24 engines each day, all hand assembled. Each highly skilled assembler builds no more than three engines per day.

THE COPO BUILD FACILTY

The COPO Build Facility, managed by Roger Allen and Rich Rinke, is located in an isolated, rural location about 50 miles north of Detroit in Oxford, Michigan. Not to be confused with the Chevrolet Performance Build Center in Wixom, where COPO and other Chevy Performance engines are assembled, the COPO Build Facility was established solely to assemble COPO Camaros. Bodies-in-white and hardware from Oshawa, engines from the Performance Build Center, supplier components such as Bogart wheels and Strange Engineering axles and

Above: The final quality assurance stage of the COPO Camaro assembly process.

Below: The assembly line for mass-produced Camaros in Oshawa, Ontario, is more complex, but still maintains the high level of Camaro build quality. Camaro quality standards must be kept, regardless of whether the car is intended for the street or the strip.

suspension pieces, as well as additional components from CCA, are sent here for final assembly.

Located so as to avoid prying eyes, the COPO Build Facility, like the Performance Build Center, more closely resembles a room in a hospital than an assembly plant.

Remarkably clean and organized, the facility consists of about two dozen work stations. As the painted bodies-in-white are received from Oshawa, they are mounted on wheeled dollies to facilitate ease of movement through the facility. Initially, the cutting away of unnecessary sheet metal and the welding of special brackets and support structures begins the transformation. Roll cages are soon welded into place. All cutting and welding operations are undertaken in one portion of the building, before the cars are wheeled into an adjoining area for assembly, first the underbody components, then drivetrain installation, and finally interior trim.

Representatives from NHRA routinely visit the facility, not only to check processes, but to certify each roll cage. The assembly pace is slow and methodical; the COPO Camaros being built here are hand crafted with the care and attention to detail afforded any low-volume super car.

Members of the COPO team place their signatures on the transmission tunnel, or elsewhere, of every COPO vehicle, both as a source of pride, not unlike an artist who signs his canvas, but also to authenticate the vehicle in case its origin is ever questioned in the future. Likewise, the owner certificate is affixed inside the trunk ahead of the fuel cell, and perhaps even unknown to the owners themselves, documentation is hidden above the headliner inside the car. Years from now, if a COPO Camaro ever changes ownership, or if a restoration takes place, or if there is any question about COPO authenticity, the proof is with the car itself.

There will be COPO clones to be sure, but authentic COPO Camaros will be cherished for decades to come.

RICK HENDRICK: ENGINE BUILDER

Of the 66 private-owner purchasers of the new COPO Camaro, 12 opted for the "Build Your Own Engine" package. For an additional $5,800, the owner could experience the opportunity to build his or her engine at the Chevrolet Performance Build Center, under the watchful eye of a skilled expert builder.

One of the COPO Camaro purchasers who checked off the "build-your-own" box was Rick Hendrick, chairman and CEO of Hendrick Motorsports and Hendrick Automotive Group. Hendrick is no stranger to competition or success, so it comes as no surprise that he expressed interest in owning the new COPO Camaro. In fact, he already owns an original COPO Camaro from 1969.

As a NASCAR team owner, Hendrick is surrounded by high-performance engines every day of the week. This comfort level was clearly evident during his build session, where he was paired with skilled engine builder Rich McBride, who normally builds experimental engines at the Build Center.

The engine Hendrick assembled, one of three he purchased with the optional Collector's Package, was the COPO 327-cubic-inch motor with the 4.0-liter Whipple supercharger, the engine that was installed in his 2012 COPO Camaro.

Above: The personalized build sheet details what processes occur at each station of engine assembly.

Above right: Hendrick installs the camshaft under the watchful eye of master builder Rich McBride.

There is nothing at all "ceremonial" about the build session; the customer actually builds the entire engine, with only verbal guidance from the experienced engine builder. In Hendrick's case, he worked with the deftness, skill and confidence of someone who has worked with engines his whole life.

It looks like you've done this before.

"A few times," replies Hendrick, with a chuckle. "When I was a kid growing up on the family farm, I fixed engines on the equipment. Then, when I was sixteen, I actually won a state-wide competition for engine trouble-shooting. I guess I know a thing or two about engines."

So why did you want to build your own engine?

"That's actually a very good question. Because this is such a rare and special car, I wanted to be a part of the process, to have real involvement in its creation. I wanted to have my fingerprints on it, to not only see firsthand the rods and pistons and cylinder heads being installed, but to do it with my own hands. What makes this car special is the COPO name, but the coolest thing is that I can be a part of it."

What do you plan to do with your COPO Camaro? Race it?

"No, I don't plan to race it. I'll maybe take it to the track and play with it a little, but not much. I have other Camaros I can go fast with. I plan to use this car to promote my Chevy stores. We can rotate it

from store to store. With a single e-mail blast, we can instantly have 500 people in the showroom because of this car. No, I don't plan to campaign it in any serious way. Mostly it will sit in my collection next to my black '69 COPO."

What do you think of the engine you just built?

"At Hendrick Motorsports we build about 700 race motors a year and I can tell you this engine is as good as any race piece I've seen. This LSX block is bullet proof."

What does COPO mean to you?

"It has a tremendous amount of heritage. The COPO, ZL1 and Z28 Camaros are the most sought after, no doubt. When a COPO shows up at auction, people go crazy. But the thing is, most of the really good COPOs never make it to auction. They're in such demand that they're usually sold privately without having to go on the auction block. COPO has such a great pedigree. There's no doubt in my mind that there will be a lot of COPO clones being built, and that's okay. But the value lies in the real thing. I have no doubt that in the years to come, a well-documented COPO or ZL1 bought today will fetch $300,000 to $500,000. That's how rare and special they are. For every ZL1 I sell, I could sell 100 more if I could just get them."

What does COPO mean to your business?

"The COPO name has a tremendous halo effect for the rest of the Camaro line-up and for every franchised dealer. I think there is always going to be a segment of people who like cars and performance. Today there are the older drag racers and gear-heads who remember what the original COPO was like. The new COPO will do the same for future generations, I'm sure. With the COPO halo, I'm sure we can sell a lot of Camaros and have even more loyal and enthusiastic owners for years to come."

Rick Hendrick is joined by Chevrolet Performance and Motorsports Vice President Jim Campbell at the conclusion of the build session.

PERFORMANCE
PERFORMAN
VEHICLES • PARTS •
SONIC
ZL1

CHAPTER EIGHT: **COPO MARKETING**

"We had a great opportunity to leverage the COPO brand equity. Sure, we wanted our COPO owners to go racing, to start to build 'buzz' out in the racing community. But the ultimate goal of the COPO project was to get people to buy performance parts. We want people to build their own COPO Camaros."

Cliff Cohen, Chevy Performance Parts Manager

Facing page: The Chevrolet Performance exhibit is literally a promotional road show of performance vehicles and parts and was an ideal way to get the COPO Camaro in front of large crowds quickly.

Above: The COPO Camaro assumed "super hero" proportions in promotional materials leading up to and including the 2011 SEMA Show.

If the goal of marketing the new COPO Camaro were simply to sell less than 70 cars, there wouldn't need to be much of a marketing effort at all. The car, once announced, immediately sold out.

"We have imposed upon ourselves a big challenge," explains Chevy Performance Marketing Manager Dr. Jamie Meyer. "Not only does the car need to live up to the great COPO heritage, it needs to educate a new generation of enthusiasts about what COPO stands for in the world of motorsports. Beyond that, the COPO

The COPO Camaro proof-of-concept car was front-and-center at Detroit's annual Woodward Dream Cruise event that drew over a million people over a weekend in August 2012.

Camaro needs to support overall Chevrolet racing initiatives and drive people to the Chevrolet Performance Parts catalog. That's a tall order."

A tall order, indeed.

The SEMA Show in November 2011 was more than a debut for the COPO Camaro concept, it was both a target event and a kick-off event for a string of marketing communication initiatives. The primary goal was to get the COPO name and the COPO proof-of-concept car in front of the right audiences.

Following SEMA, the COPO concept display traveled to the Performance Racing Industry Trade Show in Orlando, Florida, the NHRA Finals in Pomona, California, and the Barrett-Jackson Scottsdale Auction in January, 2012 all to build awareness.

In the history of the American auto industry, few names evoke the spirit of performance as does the acronym COPO. This was the foundation from which the Chevy team crafted the messaging for the 2012 COPO Camaro project.

"In those first meetings, we had representatives from engineering, marketing, the show car group," remembers Chevy Performance Parts Manager Cliff Cohen. "Our thoughts then were to build one car, an example so builders could order performance parts and build their own. Our goal was to build enthusiasm for the brand, both for Chevrolet and for Camaro."

Defining words that emerged from the early Performance Team meetings were, "power," "speed," "exclusivity," "rarity" and "legendary." As discussions started mentioning the name COPO, it soon became evident to the group that a great opportunity existed. The marketing group decided that there could not be simply a "new" COPO Camaro, but a continuation of a legend

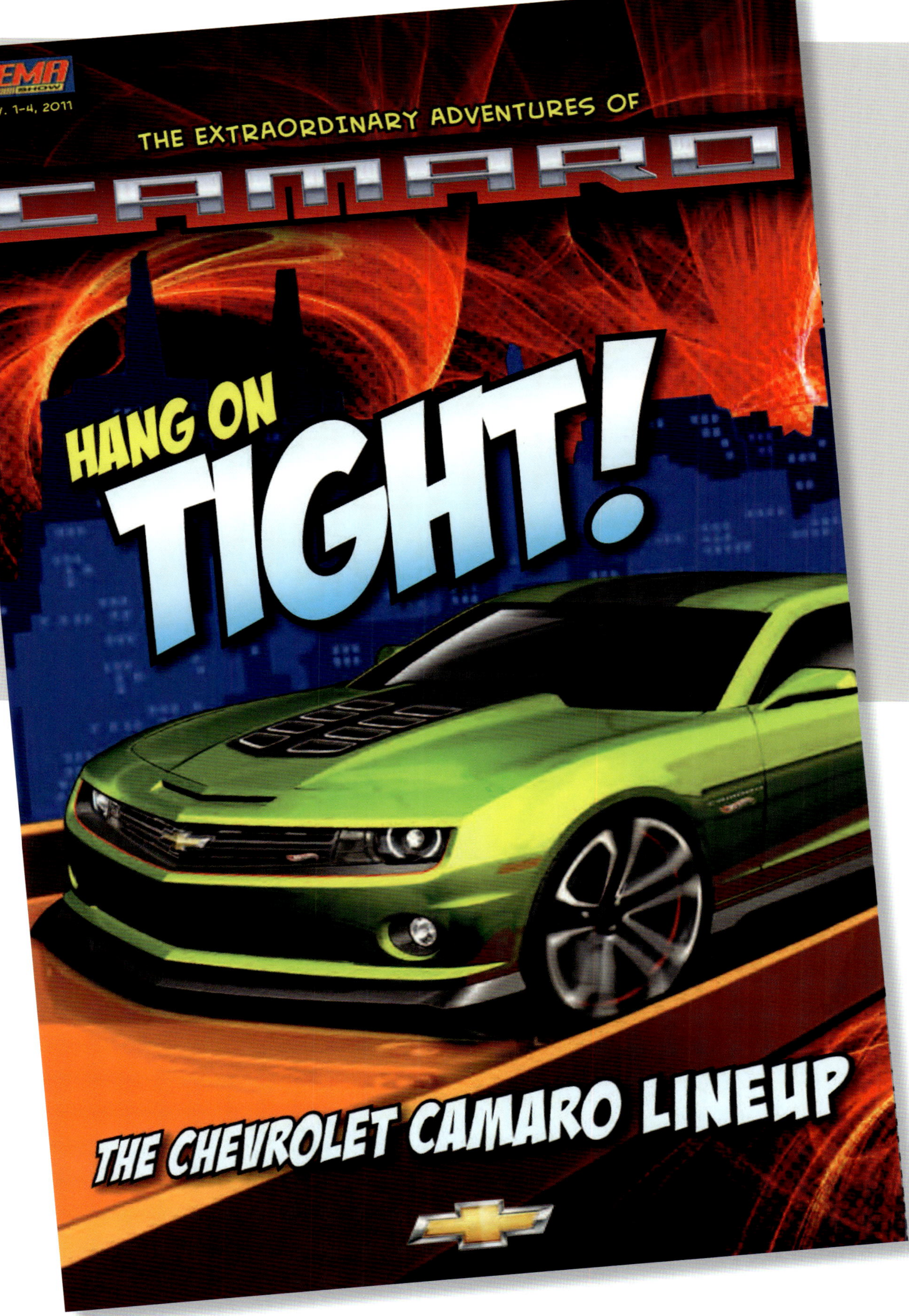

For the SEMA Show in 2011, the COPO Camaro was one of a half-dozen outrageous Camaro variants unveiled to performance-minded show-goers.

This page: The Chevy Performance Team afforded early COPO access to *Hot Rod* magazine, which resulted in a cover story where it proclaimed the COPO the "Baddest Ever!"

Facing page: The Chevy Performance Team wasted no time getting the COPO Camaro on the cover of its Performance Parts catalog, immediately putting COPO in front of an audience that understands COPO heritage and significance.

established four decades earlier.

Beginning with the SEMA Show materials, the COPO Camaro began to take on "super hero" proportions, with a comic book-like approach. This was not just any race car, the messages hinted, this was a super car.

Press releases, Chevy website information, new product fliers, brochures and the performance parts catalog all trumpeted the second coming of the COPO Camaro. The media, especially online sites and Camaro-dedicated blogs and magazines, ate the news up.

The best marketing tool of all, or course, was the first proof-of-concept car. Wherever it went, it drew interest from the right kind of people. "We wanted to get the COPO Camaro in front of people," explains Chevy Performance Director Sandor Piszar. "At several events we would fire up the engine and people would come running, like kids to a candy store. Seeing the car in real life and on the drag strip is important for visibility and image. And it's good for business."

In fact, even after the first COPO Camaros were

delivered to customers in early August 2012, the proof-of-concept Camaro was still making the rounds, notably at Detroit's famous "Woodward Dream Cruise" on August 18, an event that draws more than a million automotive enthusiasts. The COPO Camaro did what it had been doing since it was first unveiled: drawing huge crowds of interested – and envious – onlookers.

And Chevy Performance made more news at the 2012 SEMA Show, by unveiling car number 69, a COPO Camaro convertible, in a one-off color, Inferno Orange. In addition, a second production run of 2013 COPO Camaros was announced at SEMA and information was again gathered from those interested in buying a COPO. The first 2012 production run was perceived as a risk by some. With that risk now removed by the success of the 2012 edition, the second run of 69 COPO Camaros should sell out even faster than the first.

"Everything we did from a marketing perspective was aimed at conveying the legacy, the exclusivity, the performance of the COPO brand," explains Meyer. "We could not simply rely on the COPO brand as it existed four decades ago, we had to grow the brand and make it relevant to a new generation of Chevy fans."

"We had a great opportunity to leverage the COPO brand equity," says Cohen. "Sure, we wanted our COPO owners to go racing, to start to build 'buzz.' The ultimate goal of the COPO project was to get people to buy performance parts. We want people to build their own COPO Camaros. All of the necessary parts, including the body, are available in the performance parts catalog."

In addition to parts sales, the COPO brand also

Camaro Now, a magazine devoted only to fifth-generation Camaros, was on hand to witness proof-of-concept testing and get early behind-the-scenes information.

supports the entire Camaro lineup. "Camaro has always covered the full spectrum of performance, and that legacy continues today," concludes Piszar. "From modern sports car to V8 muscle car, from road course champ to drag strip winner, Camaro does it all."

The COPO Camaro was tasked with a huge challenge, and by every measure, it has succeeded.

The COPO legend continues.

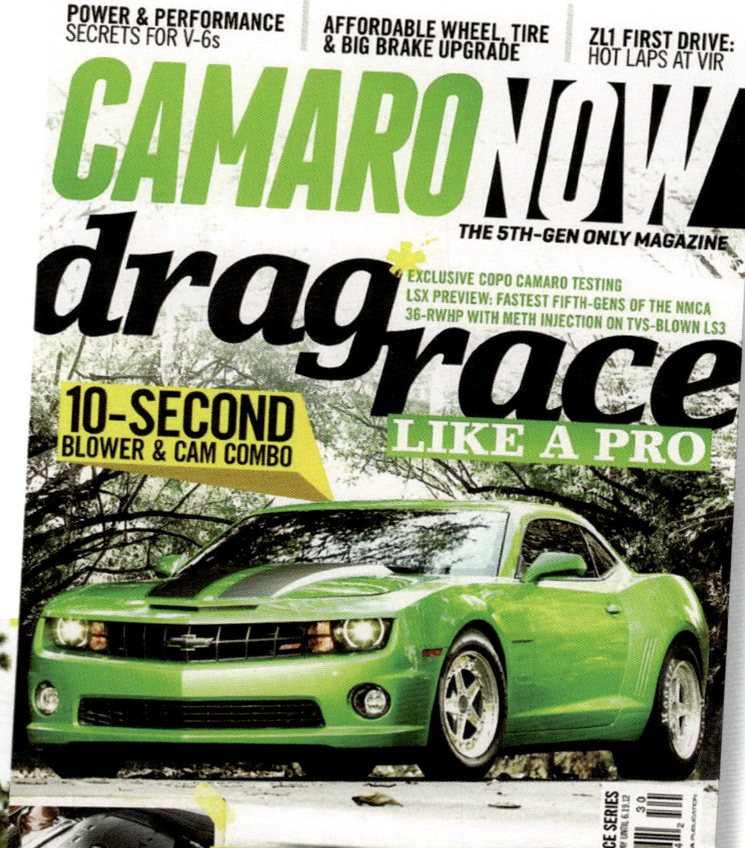

THE LEGEND LIVES

AN EXCLUSIVE LOOK INSIDE THE 2012 COPO CAMARO

BY JUSTIN CESLER // PHOTOGRAPHY BY THE AUTHOR

brakes to set it up, and plumes of tire smoke to heat the 9-inch wide hides. Out of the burnout box and into the beams, yellow yellow, onto the transbrake, and 1.40-seconds later, the COPO Camaro was on its way down track. In just 9.69-seconds it was all over. Five grueling years worth of blood, sweat, internal politics, tears, heartache, joy, and plain old hard work culminating in a 140mph blast down 1,320 feet worth of asphalt. What we had just witnessed wasn't only a track pass; it was history in the making.

To understand the COPO Camaro's importance, one must first understand where this concept came from and to do that, we've got to turn back the clocks to 1968, the second year of the Camaro, which just like today was an all-new hot selling muscle car that enthusiasts loved. Drag racing was huge and class racing was the only way to prove who was the king of the muscle cars. Unfortunately (or fortunately, depending on how you look at it), the rules of yesteryear mandated that "stock" cars had to be available to the public, in units of 50 or more, direct from the factory. Ford produced the Mustang with a 428 Cobra Jet engine, Chrysler

office scheming, Fred was 9560, which was a Central Office Production Order run that contained a special order for 50 brand new ZL1 Camaros that were to be outfitted with the 430hp aluminum ZL1 engine, borrowed from the Corvette, along with a special 4.10:1 equipped rear end and either a TH400 or Muncie four-speed transmission. Because they were going to semi-officially build 50 of these at the factory, a new class racer was born and the COPO 9560 Camaro was instantly a crowd and racer favorite at the dragstrip. In AHRA trim, Fred Gibb and partner Dick Harrell went out and ran hard, clocking a best time of 10.29 at 132mph. The COPO Camaro was real, fast, and awesome, which meant GM was back in the game and gunning for the top spot at every race it unofficially entered. Eventually, other dealers heard of this program and out of the same racing spirit that built the COPO 9560 came the COPO 9561 production order, which offered a smaller engine (among other things) at a much more affordable price. While much cheaper and more popular, it was the COPO 9560 ZL1 that held the top spot, with an eventual 69 units being built

1. Good things come to those who wait. It's been over 40 years since a brand-new COPO Camaro hit the track and its been worth the wait. With 5 years of development, the '12 COPO Camaro is finally ready to take the NHRA by storm, slow economy and big corporate fuel initiatives be damned.

2. Built specifically for NHRA Stock Eliminator AA/S class racing, the COPO team spent countless hours developing the incredible 327 ci (5.3-liter) LSX engine that you see here. Based on an LSX block, this 10.2:1 compression, fully forged engine package includes a set of LS7 cylinder heads, a Whipple 2.9-liter supercharger, and a hydraulic roller camshaft cut with 0.650-inches of lift and 244/255 degrees of duration at 0.050-inches.

3. Boost is best in the AA/S world and when competing with the Cobra Jet crowd, Chevrolet Performance wanted to do it right, using this 2.9-liter Whipple supercharger system. Pullied to make around 15 pounds of boost on the 327, the Whipple supercharger feeds off of the front mounted throttle body and is cooled by an internal air-to-water heat exchanger. Chevrolet Performance was silent on the horsepower rating but the 140 mph traps should give you a good idea of how potent this mill will be.

Chevrolet Introduces New 'COPO' Camaro

Concept evokes the spirit of special-order models for Stock Eliminator competition

LAS VEGAS, October 31, 2011 – The COPO Camaro is back at Chevrolet, as a concept designed to the specifications for NHRA Stock Eliminator drag racing competition.

"The COPO Camaro is a proof of concept for what a Chevrolet Stock Eliminator entry could look like," said Jim Campbell, GM U.S. vice president of Performance Vehicles and Motorsports. "And it is a clear indication that Chevrolet intends to homologate the Camaro for sportsman drag racing."

The COPO concept vehicle is designed to accommodate more than one engine option, including a naturally aspirated 427 engine (7.0L) – the same displacement as the original COPO Camaros from 1969 – and a supercharged 327 (5.3L) engine. Among the many racing-specific features and equipment is a conversion from the Camaro's standard independent rear axle to a solid axle, as well as a full chrome moly roll cage.

The COPO Legacy

Since 1955, NHRA Stock Eliminator has been a straight-line proving ground for the quickest cars to come out of Detroit. Within Stock Eliminator, there are many classes, all defined by the ratio of vehicle shipping weight and the assigned horsepower factor. Because of this tightly monitored set of rules and historically brutal competition, Stock Eliminator is the ultimate test for factory muscle cars.

From the "Fuelie" '57 Bel Air to the '62 409 Impala and countless muscle cars that came later, Chevrolet has enjoyed a long, dominant position in this sportsman drag racing category. None of the cars, however, have dominated both the track and muscle car folklore like the legendary COPO Camaros produced in 1969.

In the '60s, COPO was the acronym for Central Office Production Order, within Chevrolet's vehicle special-order program. Although normally used for fleet orders of trucks and company-owned cars, it was manipulated by a few performance-minded dealers to order vehicles with larger engines than were available in regular-production models – mostly with the intent of getting them to Stock Eliminator racers.

By pushing Chevrolet's Central Office Production Order special-order program to its limit, a number of dealers were able to get 427-cubic-inch big-block engines installed in a handful of Camaros, when the largest official engine available was a 396. Two versions of the 427 engine were wrangled out of the factory: COPO 9561 was the Corvette-based L-72 edition with an iron cylinder block and COPO 9560 was the racing-designed ZL1 engine with a lighter aluminum cylinder block.

The COPO Camaros opened up the NHRA rulebook to some exciting combinations for Camaro, helping keep Chevrolet at the top of the ultra-competitive form of motorsports. In fact, they were not only competitive in NHRA Stock Eliminator when new, but still hold the national ET and MPH records in several classes.

Racing enthusiasts who are interested in more information can go to www.gmperformanceparts.com to sign up for COPO Camaro concept updates.

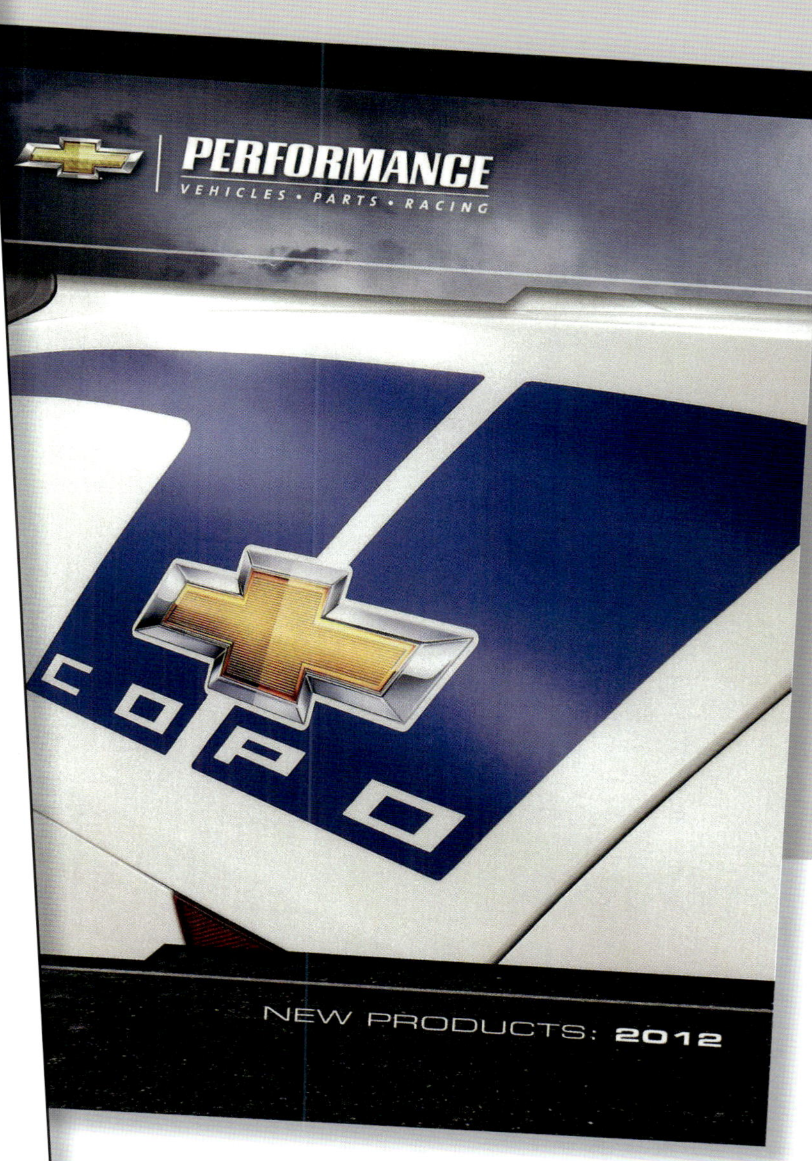

The Chevy Performance Team kept the media informed every step of the way with well-timed press releases.

Chevrolet COPO Camaro Goes From Concept to Production

Stock Eliminator drag racer the quickest Camaro ever offered by Chevrolet

DETROIT, March 8, 2012 – Chevrolet will build 69 COPO Camaros for 2012, the brand's first purpose-built Camaro drag-racing specialty car designed to compete with the quickest in NHRA's Stock Eliminator and Super Stock classes. National records for quarter-mile times in these contests are in the nine-second range.

As such, the COPO Camaros are expected to be the quickest Camaro ever offered by Chevrolet.

"The COPO Camaro is going to shake up the sportsman drag racing ranks this summer and give Chevy fans a great new reason to cheer on the Bowtie," said Jim Campbell, GM U.S. vice president of Performance Vehicles & Motorsports. "COPO builds off the strengths that have made the Camaro the best-selling sports car in America. And while it was developed strictly for the drag strip, the COPO Camaro is infused with the same performance pedigree that every Camaro shares."

The 69-car production for the 2012 COPO Camaro matches the number of "ZL-1" COPO Camaros made in 1969. COPO stands for Central Office Production Order and was Chevrolet's special-order system in used by dealers to build high-performance models in the 1960s.

The new COPO Camaros will be built using factory "body-in-white" body structures produced at the Oshawa, Ontario plant that manufactures regular-production Camaros. They are the same body-in-white body shells available to all racers under Chevrolet Performance part number 19243374.

Customers will order and complete the transaction for their COPO Camaro at their preferred Chevrolet dealer with delivery at the General Motors Performance Build Center in Wixom, Mich.

Deliveries will begin early this summer.

Highlights of the new COPO Camaro program include:

- A sequenced build number matched to the engine but sold without a Vehicle Identification Number and cannot be registered for highway use
- Three racing-class engine are available, including a naturally aspirated 427 (7.0L) and two supercharged 327 (5.3L) V-8 engines
- Engine assembly at GM's Performance Build Center, where the buyer can opt to participate in the engine assembly similar to Chevrolet's Corvette Engine Build Experience and the Chevrolet Performance Build Your Own Crate Engine programs
- Engines pairing with a Powerglide automatic transmission designed for drag racing
- Five colors: Black, Summit White, Victory Red, Silver Ice Metallic and Ashen Gray Metallic
- A COPO graphics package similar to the one introduced on the concept vehicle available in Metallic White, Flat Black, Inferno Orange Metallic and Chevy Racing Blue
- Pricing starting at $89,000
- A special collector's package offering the purchase of all three engines with the COPO Camaro – including one installed in the car at delivery – with each engine serial number matched to the car Selection process

The COPO Camaro concept was first shown at the 2011 Specialty Equipment Market Association (SEMA) show in Las Vegas, where the overwhelming response by more than 2,000 racing enthusiasts shaped the decision to produce a limited number of COPO Camaros.

To ensure fair access to the limited number of COPO Camaros, an independent third party was used to identify the first individuals who would be offered the opportunity to buy one of the new COPO Camaros. Those selected will receive a confirmation letter with instructions on how to fulfill the purchase contract, choose the engine option for their intended racing class, and take delivery.

Designed to win

The COPO Camaro is designed to NHRA racing specifications including a solid axle and a full chrome moly roll cage. Inside, most of the standard sound deadening and power accessories have been deleted in order to optimize weight for NHRA racing. Also included is a pair of racing bucket seats (no rear seat), a safety harness for the driver, a competition floor shifter and Chevrolet Performance gauges.

The three engines offered in the COPO Camaro program were developed to align with the top classes in NHRA's various Stock Eliminator and Super Stock ranks. They are:

- An LS7-based naturally aspirated 427 (7.0L) V-8
- A supercharged, LSX-based 327 (5.3L) V-8 featuring a 2.9L supercharger
- A supercharged, LSX-based 327 (5.3L) V-8 featuring a 4.0L supercharger

The 2012 COPO Camaro is being offered as a performance part, with a specific part number (P/N 20129562). It cannot be registered, titled, licensed, or driven on public roads or highways. COPO is specifically offered for off-highway, competitive NHRA use only.

Wherever the proof-of-concept car traveled with the Chevrolet Performance exhibit, it drew interest among enthusiasts wanting to get a closer look at the "new COPO."

Rick Hendrick Builds Custom Engine for 2012 COPO Camaro

Motorsports legend revved up about high-performance drag racing

WIXOM, Mich., June 26, 2012 – Rick Hendrick, owner of NASCAR team Hendrick Motorsports and chairman of Hendrick Automotive Group, built the engine for his 2012 COPO Camaro at General Motors' Performance Build Center today, as part of Chevrolet's series of customer engine build experiences.

In 2011, Hendrick also took part in Chevrolet's Corvette engine build experience.

"Last year's Corvette engine build was such a memorable experience that I couldn't pass up the opportunity to do it again with a COPO Camaro. As a Chevy enthusiast and collector, it's a real privilege to do something like this," Hendrick said. "I want to thank everyone at the Performance Build Center for having me back. It means so much to spend time with people who share my passion for cars and work so hard to produce some of the best engines in the world."

In addition to the Corvette Engine Build Experience and COPO Engine Build Experience, Chevrolet also has a Crate Engine Build Experience. These engine-building opportunities offer customers the convenience and assurance of purchasing a factory-engineered performance engine with the personal satisfaction of building one's own engine for a project vehicle.

"Building an engine is a time-honored tradition in hot rodding, and this program allows enthusiasts to enjoy that magical do-it-yourself feeling, while still enjoying the value of a GM Powertrain-engineered and factory-warrantied engine," said Jim Campbell, GM U.S. vice president of Performance Vehicles and Motorsports. "For hands-on hot rodders, these programs truly enable them to say they did it all when it came to building their project. There's nothing else like it in the industry."

In March, Chevrolet announced it will build 69 COPO Camaros for 2012, the brand's first purpose-built Camaro drag-racing specialty car designed to compete with the quickest in NHRA's Stock Eliminator and Super Stock classes. National records for quarter-mile times in these contests are in the nine-second range. As such, the COPO Camaros are expected to be the quickest Camaros ever offered by Chevrolet.

"The COPO Camaro is going to shake up the sportsman drag racing ranks this summer and give Chevy fans a great new reason to cheer on the Bow-tie," Campbell said. "COPO builds off the strengths that have made the Camaro the best-selling sports car in America. And while it was developed strictly for the drag strip, the COPO Camaro is infused with the same performance pedigree that every Camaro shares."

The 69-car production for the 2012 COPO Camaro matches the number of "ZL-1" COPO Camaros made in 1969. COPO stands for Central Office Production Order and was Chevrolet's special-order system used by dealers to build high-performance models in the 1960s.

The new COPO Camaros will be built using factory "body-in-white" body structures produced at the Oshawa, Ontario plant that manufactures regular-production Camaros. They are the same body-in-white body shells available to all racers under Chevrolet Performance part number 19243374.

DOWN & DIRTY

DETAILS ABOUT THE COPO CAMARO

You've seen the 2012 COPO Camaro topless. Now, get to know this racing beauty a little better.

2 **COPO WAS A SPECIAL-ORDER DESIGNATION** used for special equipment packages, primarily for small batch fleet customer packages.

3 **A FEW DEALERS CLEVERLY MANIPULATED** small batch COPO orders to stuff Corvette engines into Camaros.

4 **IN 1969, THREE SPECIAL COPO PACKAGES** were built designated by codes #9560, #9561 and #9737.

5 **OF THE COPO LEGACY,** order #9560 became the benchmark 1969 COPO Camaro ZL1 (only 69 were built.)

6 **BY PUSHING THE SPECIAL-ORDER PROGRAM** to its limit, a number of dealers were able to get 427 cu.-in. big-block engines installed in a handful of 1969 Camaros. (A 396 cu.-in. was the largest official engine available for Camaro at the time.)

Next four pages: An excerpt from the 2012 "Chevrolet at SEMA" brochure highlighting everything you need to know about COPO Camaros old and new.

7 **COPO #9560 AND COPO #9561** were essentially the same car, but COPO 9560 had one big difference — the engine was the all-aluminum ZL1.

8 **COPO #9561 GOT YOU** an iron-block engine.

9 **COPO #9737 WAS THE SPORTS CAR CONVERSION** with either engine available, a 140-mph speedometer and 15 x 7 Rally wheels.

10 **ALL 1969 COPO CAMAROS** were emissions-certified, carried both the 12/12 and 5/50 warranties, and were street legal.

11 **UNLIKE OTHER RACE-ONLY EXOTICS,** a 1969 COPO Camaro was a true dual-purpose machine. It had the hardware to win at the track and the presence to turn heads at the drive-in.

12 **THE 1969 COPO CAMAROS OPENED UP** the National Hot Rod Association (NHRA) Rulebook to some exciting combinations for Camaro, helping keep Chevrolet at the top of the ultra-competitive form of motorsports.

13 **SOME 1969 COPO CAMAROS STILL HOLD** the national ET and mph records in several NHRA Stock Eliminator classes.

14 **NATIONAL RECORDS FOR QUARTER-MILE TIMES** in Stock Eliminator and Super Stock contests are in the seven- to nine-second range.

15 **MANY MUSCLE CAR COLLECTORS** consider the 1969 COPO Camaro a Blue Chip investment.

16 **THE 2012 COPO CAMARO** was first shown as a concept at last year's SEMA Show. (Just a refresher, in case you've been living under a rock. Or cryogenically frozen. Or whatever it is that folks are doing these days.)

SEE MORE AT TheBLOCK

1

COPO IS GM SHORTHAND FOR CENTRAL OFFICE PRODUCTION ORDER.

ONLY TWO CONVERTIBLE MODELS WILL BE PRODUCED IN THE 2012 MODEL RUN.

DOWN & DIRTY

DETAILS ABOUT THE COPO CAMARO (CONTINUED)

17 **HOT ROD ENTHUSIASTS** who work at the Performance Build Center in Wixom, Mich., developed the 2012 concept after hours.

18 **THE OVERWHELMING RESPONSE** by more than 3,000 racing enthusiasts shaped Chevrolet's decision to produce a limited number for the 2012 model year.

19 **A 69-CAR PRODUCTION** was selected to commemorate the original number of ZL-1 COPO Camaros made in 1969.

20 **A MINIMUM OF 50** vehicles needed to be produced to qualify it for NHRA competition.

21 **THE LIMITED PRODUCTION** makes these cars a rarity. But you can actually build your own version using Chevrolet Performance parts. (Check out the sidebar.)

22 **THE COPO METHODOLOGY** was reinstituted for the 2012 production run.

23 **TODAY'S COPO CAMAROS** are being offered as a performance part with a specific part number (20129562).

24 **THE PART NUMBER IS** a continuation of the heritage of the COPO Camaros from 1969.

25 **UNLIKE ITS PREDECESSOR,** the 2012 COPO Camaro is fully endorsed by Chevrolet Performance.

26 **IT'S CHEVROLET'S FIRST** purpose-built Camaro drag-racing specialty car.

27 **IT'S DESIGNED** to NHRA racing specifications.

28 **IT'S EXPECTED TO BE** the quickest Camaro ever offered by Chevrolet.

29 **EVERY STEP OF THE BUILD** at the Chevrolet Performance COPO Camaro assembly facility ensures identical high quality.

30 **THE 2012** COPO Camaros were built using factory body-in-white body structures.

31 **THE SAME BODY-IN-WHITE SHELLS** are available to all racers from Chevrolet Performance (19243374).

32 **THE BODY-IN-WHITE** includes an assembled body structure — front fenders, hood, roof, doors, rear quarters and trunk lid — and it comes with the complete floor pans and chassis rails.

33 **THE FINISH DETAIL** on the 2012 COPO Camaro — right down to the blackout re-spray of the underbody and engine compartment — is show quality.

34 **TO ENSURE FAIR ACCESS,** an independent third party identified who was offered the opportunity to buy a 2012 COPO Camaro.

35 **A 2012 COPO CAMARO** starts at $89,000.

36 **OF THE 69 2012 COPO CAMAROS** produced, only two are convertibles — serial numbers 68 and 69.

37 **SERIAL NUMBER 68** is the first new COPO Camaro with a manual transmission.

38 **IT RESIDES AT** the GM Heritage Center in metro Detroit.

39 **THE 2012 COPO CAMARO** convertible shown at this year's SEMA Show is serial number 69. (Go take a look at it.)

40 **SERIAL NUMBER 69** is the last of a sequenced number build matched to the engine.

41 **THE ENGINE SOUNDS** absolutely angry. In fact, its roar can scare the snot out of a grown man. (We know. We've done it.)

42 **THE NHRA HAS RATED** the 327 engine with the 4.0L supercharger at 550 horsepower.

43 **RECOMMENDED MAX** engine RPM is 7500.

44 **THE ENGINE WAS HAND ASSEMBLED** by one worker from start to finish at the Performance Build Center in Wixom, Mich.

45 **SERIAL NUMBER 69** is the first new COPO Camaro with a 3-speed automatic transmission.

46 **THE TRANSMISSION** is designed specifically for drag racing.

47 **OTHER PARTS** include an Aeromotive "Eliminator" fuel pump and a Hurst Quarter Stick® three-speed automatic shifter.

48 **IT RIDES ON** Bogart Racing lightweight wheels with unique COPO engraving and 30-in. x 9-in. x 15-in. radial slicks and skinny front drag tires.

57

THE PANTONE COLOR INSTITUTE® NAMED INFERNO ORANGE (AKA PANTONE® 17-1463 TANGERINE TANGO) THE COLOR OF THE YEAR FOR 2012. *(Only the best for this car.)*

49

THE 2012 COPO CAMARO HAS A SUPERCHARGED, LSX-BASED 327 (5.3L) V8 ENGINE FEATURING A 4.0L SUPERCHARGER.

50 **IT'S THE ONLY** 2012 COPO Camaro offered in an Inferno Orange exterior.

51 **ITS INTERIOR HAS** Inferno Orange accents as well.

52 **IT HAS** no rear seat.

53 **THERE IS A PAIR** of racing buckets seats.

54 **THERE'S ALSO A SAFETY HARNESS** for the driver and a competition floor shifter.

55 **IT HAS CHEVROLET** Performance gauges by Auto Meter with the gold Bowtie logo on the dials.

56

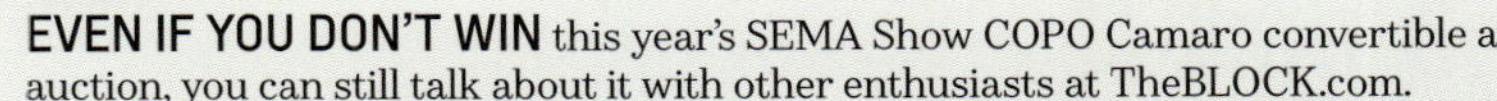

EVEN IF YOU DON'T WIN this year's SEMA Show COPO Camaro convertible at auction, you can still talk about it with other enthusiasts at TheBLOCK.com.

58 **IT HAS** a solid axle.

59 **IT ALSO HAS** a full chrome moly roll cage.

60 **THE MOLY CAGE** has been NHRA-certified to 8.50 ET.

61 **INSIDE, MOST OF** the standard sound deadening and power accessories have been deleted to optimize weight for NHRA racing.

62 **IT WILL BE AUCTIONED AT** Barrett-Jackson's West World of Scottsdale event in Arizona this coming January. (Slim chance you're going to win that bidding war.)

63 **ITS PROCEEDS WILL BENEFIT** the American Heart Association.

64 **IT'S BEING SOLD** without a Vehicle Identification Number (VIN).

65 **NO VIN MEANS** it can't be registered, titled, licensed or driven on public roads or highways. (Who cares. This is a car meant for off-highway, competitive NHRA use anyway).

66 **THE NHRA LETS CLONE** cars compete, and with components from Chevrolet Performance you can build your own modern-day COPO Camaro. (Did we mention that already?)

67 **CHEVROLET PERFORMANCE** also offers a build book to help you piece together your own Gen 5 COPO Camaro.

68 **THE CONVERTIBLE TOP** on serial numbers 68 and 69 is fully operational.

69 **THE COPO LEGACY CONTINUES** Chevrolet Performance just announced that there will be a 2013 COPO production run. (Chevrolet enthusiasts demanded it and we listened).

SPEC CHECK

BUILD YOUR OWN COPO

IF YOU WEREN'T ONE OF THE LUCKY FEW TO BUY A COMPLETE COPO CAMARO FOR 2012, YOU CAN STILL BUILD YOUR OWN. CHEVROLET PERFORMANCE HAS A FULL LINE OF COPO PARTS AND ACCESSORIES THAT HAVE BEEN ENGINEERED, TESTED AND PROVEN FOR YOUR FIFTH-GENERATION CAMARO, INCLUDING:

- COPO LS7 aluminum cylinder block (19213580)
- COPO LS7 aluminum cylinder heads (12578449)
- COPO LSX ignition controller (19171130)
- COPO Camaro body-in-white (19243374)

THERE'S EVEN A BUILD BOOK THAT TELLS YOU HOW TO PUT IT ALL TOGETHER. SHOP FOR THEM ONLINE AT CHEVROLETPERFORMANCE.COM OR VISIT YOUR LOCAL PERFORMANCE DEALER. ENJOY, BOWTIE FANS.

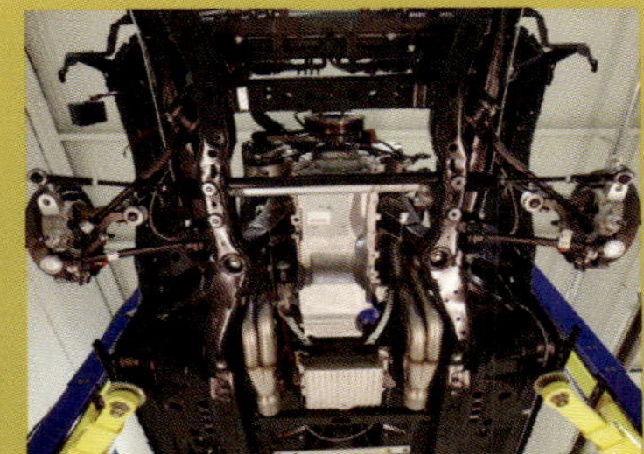

COPO

CHAPTER NINE: **THE ENTHUSIASTS**

"We were sitting around a table with a speaker phone in the center. We had the list of potential buyers. Before we made the first call, we looked at each other somewhat hesitantly. How many calls would we have to make to find less than seventy customers? But when our first twelve calls resulted in twelve sales without hesitation, we knew something very special was happening."

Dr. Jamie Meyer, Chevrolet Performance Marketing Manager

At the 2011 SEMA Show in Las Vegas, the COPO Camaro Concept was there to gauge the reaction from show-goers. Wisely, the Chevrolet Performance staff went a step further. They distributed a brief questionnaire asking for contact information, interest in purchasing a COPO, drag-racing experience, etc. It is one thing for someone to say they like the COPO Camaro; it's quite another for someone to say they would actually buy one!

When the Chevy team returned to Detroit, they e-mailed business reply cards to everyone who had filled out a form. Between the SEMA Show, the Performance Racing Industry Show, Barrett-Jackson and a few NHRA races, an impressive 3,200 replies came back.

Remembers Performance Marketing Manager Dr. Jamie Meyer: "We had a daunting task in front of us. How were we going to whittle that list down to about sixty customers?"

As it turned out, Chevy Performance couldn't, nor wouldn't, attempt it. After consulting with Chevy

Facing page: The COPO Camaro no. 7 of Jim Boburka, sporting a new grill from the Chevy Performance Parts catalog. Boburka was careful to preserve the COPO logo.

Left: The first four COPO Camaros are staged for customer delivery at the Chevrolet Performance Build Center in Wixom, Michigan.

"Build it.
We will come."

management and the GM legal staff, it was decided to have an independent, third-party research firm do the job. This way, Chevy would stay at arm's length from the selection process. The overriding intent of Chevrolet Performance was to treat its loyal enthusiasts and Chevy dealers fairly.

The research firm sent a survey to the candidates and asked them a series of questions: Are you still interested? What color would you choose? What engine do you prefer? What transmission?

Once survey responses were returned, the research firm contacted the group once more. This time, the survey asked the candidates if they planned to store the car or race it. Chevy management knew that some purchases would be as investments, or as a part of a larger automotive collection, but they also wanted many cars out on the track racing. After all, that was what the COPO Camaro was designed to do: build grassroots racing interest and sell COPO-related performance parts.

Further, candidates were asked if they had NHRA or other drag racing experience, or some kind of 1969 COPO Camaro experience. There was a space for unsolicited comments, so that candidates could express verbally why they felt they should be selected.

"This is something Chevrolet really needs to do," wrote one respondent. "Chevy is conspicuous in its absence. This car will bring the Chevrolet nameplate back into the forefront of NHRA class racing."

"Please bring back the heritage of our beloved Camaro with a state-of-the-art COPO version," wrote another.

"I currently crew on a Mustang Cobra Jet team and I would like to race my own car," stated another. "Camaro

is my choice."

"I would sell my 2009 Dodge Drag Pak!" exclaimed another.

Added yet another, "Build it. We will come."

One respondent minced no words. "I think Chevy should get out there and kick butt!"

Perhaps no one was more emphatic than another respondent, who said, simply, "BUILD IT!!!!!!!!!!!!!!!!!!!!!!!!!!" with no fewer than 26 exclamation points.

And there was one final question: Are you in a position to buy the COPO Camaro now?

After this step, the research firm presented the list to Chevrolet Performance in ranked order, from top to bottom.

The ground rules for the Chevy team were these: Begin calling candidates from the top of the list and work their way down. As soon as the cars were sold, the

Left: Much to the chagrin of GM Security, owner Jim Boburka burns rubber departing the Chevrolet Performance Build Center.

Above: Boburka loading his new COPO Camaro (serial no. 7).

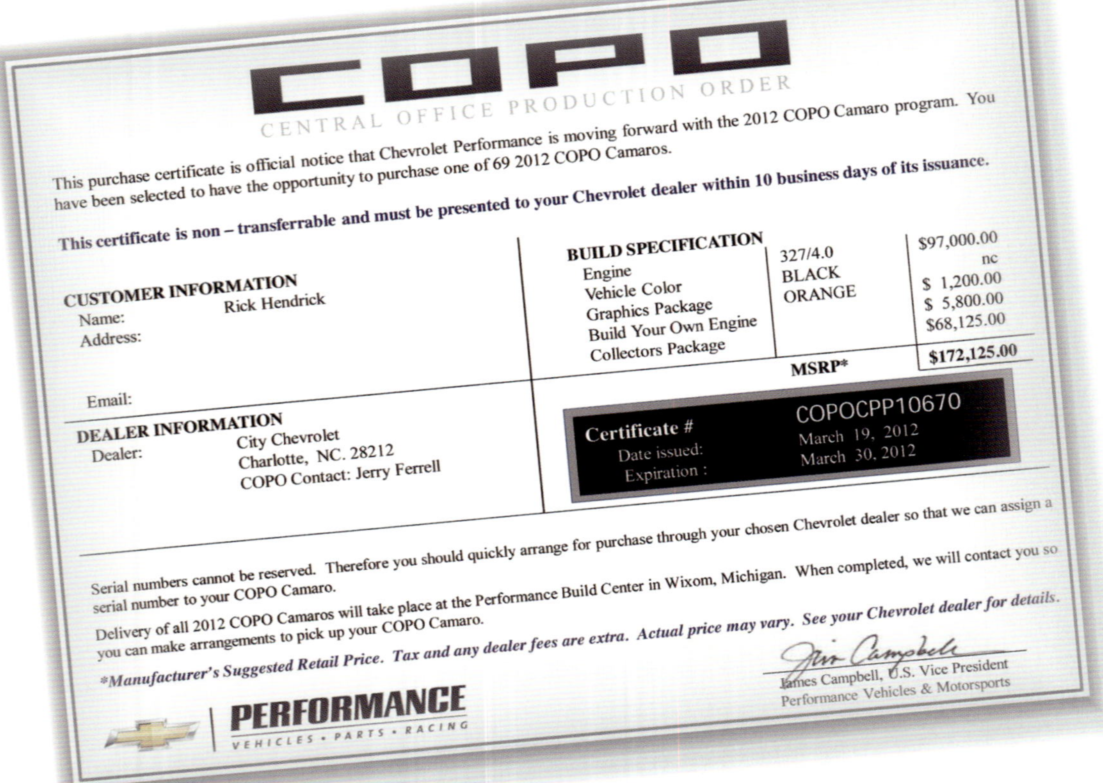

COPO

CENTRAL OFFICE PRODUCTION ORDER

This purchase certificate is official notice that Chevrolet Performance is moving forward with the 2012 COPO Camaro program. You have been selected to have the opportunity to purchase one of 69 2012 COPO Camaros.

This certificate is non – transferrable and must be presented to your Chevrolet dealer within 10 business days of its issuance.

CUSTOMER INFORMATION
Name: Rick Hendrick
Address:

Email:

DEALER INFORMATION
Dealer: City Chevrolet
Charlotte, NC. 28212
COPO Contact: Jerry Ferrell

BUILD SPECIFICATION		
Engine	327/4.0	$97,000.00
Vehicle Color	BLACK	nc
Graphics Package	ORANGE	$ 1,200.00
Build Your Own Engine		$ 5,800.00
Collectors Package		$68,125.00
	MSRP*	**$172,125.00**

Certificate # COPOCPP10670
Date issued: March 19, 2012
Expiration : March 30, 2012

Serial numbers cannot be reserved. Therefore you should quickly arrange for purchase through your chosen Chevrolet dealer so that we can assign a serial number to your COPO Camaro.

Delivery of all 2012 COPO Camaros will take place at the Performance Build Center in Wixom, Michigan. When completed, we will contact you so you can make arrangements to pick up your COPO Camaro.

**Manufacturer's Suggested Retail Price. Tax and any dealer fees are extra. Actual price may vary. See your Chevrolet dealer for details.*

James Campbell, U.S. Vice President
Performance Vehicles & Motorsports

PERFORMANCE
VEHICLES • PARTS • RACING

Above: Every COPO buyer received this COPO purchase certificate confirming their ownership. In addition to receiving a paper copy, another laminated version was affixed inside the trunk of each COPO Camaro. This certificate belongs to Rick Hendrick of Hendrick Motorsports.

calling would stop. If for whatever reason a candidate dropped out after initially accepting, the very next name on the list would be contacted.

The team gathered in Vice President Jim Campbell's office, which had a conference table and a speaker phone. The calling team consisted of Meyer, Performance Team Assistant Manager Steve Johnson and Performance Parts Marketing Manager Cliff Cohen. There was a tense, yet excited mood in the room that morning.

"We were sitting around a table with a speaker phone in the center," recalls Meyer. "We had the list of potential buyers. Before we made the first call, we looked at each other somewhat nervously. How many calls would we have to make to find less than seventy customers? But when our first twelve calls resulted in twelve sales without hesitation, we knew something very special was happening."

Of the 69 COPO Camaros, there are 69 distinct stories of why their owners wanted one. Several owners had owned, or currently own, a '69 COPO Camaro and they wanted the next-generation example. One buyer had intended to buy a COPO Camaro in 1969, but instead went to serve his country in Vietnam, dashing any hopes of owning one. Until now.

One buyer's wife answered the initial phone call from the Performance Team and turned down the offer. Fortunately, she notified her husband, who quickly returned the call, wondering if he had missed the opportunity of a lifetime. He hadn't.

Another buyer is encouraging and sponsoring his 18-year-old son to get into drag racing and a factory-built COPO Camaro seemed like the perfect vehicle with which to do so.

Yet another candidate hesitated slightly on whether to purchase a COPO Camaro, explaining that he had to

Right: The COPO Camaro (serial no. 3) of Paul Cambria loaded for its trip to New Jersey.

PERFORMANCE
VEHICLES • PARTS • RACING

2012 COPO Camaro Concept

Continue to receive information about this history re-making race machine.

First Name ______ Last Name ______
City ______ State ______ ZIP Code ______
Email Address ______
Phone Number (optional) ______
Contact Preference: Email ☐ Phone ☐
Drag Racing Experience: YES ☐ NO ☐
NHRA License? (optional) YES ☐ NO ☐
NHRA License # (optional) ______
Stock Eliminator Class History? (optional) YES ☐ NO ☐
If yes, please briefly explain.

first learn whether his home in Texas had survived a tornado before he could commit. It did, and he did.

Once learning that the COPO project was going to happen, one candidate sent a polite e-mail to Chevrolet every week requesting to purchase one. Did his persistence help? Most likely not, but it apparently didn't hurt either.

A number of Camaros went to well-known racing teams. Hendrick. Vasser. Cagnazzi. Lingenfelter. Husky. ATI. And, of course, many more went to strong, independent grassroots teams.

Agreeing to buy a COPO Camaro was a decision not made lightly. For starters, the car could only be raced. It did not carry a vehicle identification number, or VIN, and was not street legal. Further, the suggested retail price (MSRP) ranged from $89,000 for the COPO Camaro installed with the 427 naturally aspirated engine, to $97,000 for the 327 4.0-liter supercharged screamer, although the final price would be determined between the delivering Chevy dealer and the customer.

For those who chose the "Build Your Own Engine" package, tack on another $5,800. Ordering the Collector's Package, which included all three available engines with matching serial numbers, the price went up another $69,000 or more, depending upon which engine was installed in the car.

Of the 66 privately-purchased COPO Camaros (serial numbers 1 and 68 remain in the possession of Chevrolet and number 69 was created for the 2012 SEMA Show), 12 opted to build their own engines at the Performance Build Center. Eight maximized their investment by purchasing all three engines. The suggested retail prices, including all options, stretched from $89,000 to $172,125. Of the total COPO build of 69 cars, the selections are as follows:

Above left: Paul Cambria was the very first owner to take delivery of a 2012 COPO Camaro on August 8, 2012. Cambria actually cancelled an order for a Mustang Cobra Jet when he learned he had been selected to purchase a new COPO Camaro.

Above: This simple questionnaire was distributed at the SEMA Show and other venues to determine interest in the new COPO Camaro.

2012 COPO CAMARO ORDER SUMMARY

OPTIONS	Number	Percentage
Ordered with 427 engine	42	55 %
Ordered with 327 2.9-liter supercharger	6	9 %
Ordered with 327 4.0-liter supercharger	20	32 %
"Build Your Own Engine"	12	22 %
Collector's Package	8	9 %

BODY COLOR		
Summit White	31	46%
Black	20	30 %
Victory Red	12	18 %
Ashen Gray Metallic	2	3 %
Silver Ice Metallic	2	3 %
Inferno Orange (Special SEMA car, not available for customer order)	1	1%

STRIPE COLOR		
Chevy Racing Blue	23	34 %
Flat Black	15	22 %
Inferno Orange	11	16 %
Metallic White	7	10 %
Stripe Deleted	12	18 %

SERIAL NO. 1 (Proof of Concept)

Body Style:	Coupe
Color:	White
Graphics:	Chevy Racing Blue (pre-production design)
Engine:	427, 327/4.0 SC, 327/2.9 SC (all 3 engines rotated for testing)
Transmission:	Powerglide

Build Own Engine Package:	No
Collectors' Package Engines:	No
Owner:	Chevrolet
Dealer:	None

SERIAL NO. 2

Body Style:	Coupe
Color:	Black
Graphics:	Inferno Orange
Engine:	327/4.0 SC
Transmission:	Powerglide
Build Own Engine Package:	Yes
Collectors' Package Engines:	427, 327/2.9 SC
Dealer:	City Chevrolet, Charlotte, NC

SERIAL NO. 3

Body Style:	Coupe
Color:	Black
Graphics:	Flat Black
Engine:	327/4.0 SC
Transmission:	Powerglide
Build Own Engine Package:	No
Collectors' Package Engines:	No
Dealer:	Paddock Chevrolet, Kenmore, NJ

SERIAL NO. 4

Body Style:	Coupe	**Build Own Engine Package:**	No
Color:	Summit White	**Collectors' Package Engines:**	427, 327/4.0 SC
Graphics:	No	**Dealer:**	Jimmy Vasser Chevrolet, Napa, CA
Engine:	327/2.9 SC		
Transmission:	Powerglide		

SERIAL NO. 5

Body Style:	Coupe	**Build Own Engine Package:**	Yes
Color:	Summit White	**Collectors' Package Engines:**	327/2.9 SC, 327/4.0 SC
Graphics:	Chevy Racing Blue	**Dealer:**	Berger Chevrolet, Grand Rapids, MI
Engine:	427		
Transmission:	Powerglide		

SERIAL NO. 6

Body Style:	Coupe	**Build Own Engine Package:**	No
Color:	Summit White	**Collectors' Package Engines:**	No
Graphics:	No	**Dealer:**	Carter Chevrolet, Shelby, NC
Engine:	427		
Transmission:	Powerglide		

SERIAL NO. 7

Body Style:	Coupe	**Build Own Engine Package:**	No
Color:	Victory Red	**Collectors' Package Engines:**	No
Graphics:	No	**Dealer:**	Jim Crivelli Chevrolet, Pittsburgh, PA
Engine:	427		
Transmission:	Powerglide		

SERIAL NO. 8

Body Style:	Coupe
Color:	Summit White
Graphics:	No
Engine:	327/4.0 SC
Transmission:	Powerglide
Build Own Engine Package:	No
Collectors' Package Engines:	No
Dealer:	Jim Crivelli Chevrolet, McKees Rocks, PA

SERIAL NO. 9

Body Style:	Coupe
Color:	Summit White
Graphics:	Inferno Orange
Engine:	327/4.0 SC
Transmission:	Powerglide
Build Own Engine Package:	No
Collectors' Package Engines:	No
Dealer:	Kerbeck Chevrolet, Atlantic City, NJ

SERIAL NO. 10

Body Style:	Coupe
Color:	Summit White
Graphics:	Chevy Racing Blue
Engine:	327/4.0 SC
Transmission:	Powerglide
Build Own Engine Package:	No
Collectors' Package Engines:	No
Dealer:	NA

SERIAL NO. 11

Body Style:	Coupe
Color:	Black
Graphics:	Inferno Orange
Engine:	427
Transmission:	Powerglide
Build Own Engine Package:	No
Collectors' Package Engines:	No
Dealer:	Bill McCurley Chevrolet, Pasco, WA

SERIAL NO. 12

Body Style:	Coupe	**Build Own Engine Package:**	No
Color:	Victory Red	**Collectors' Package Engines:**	No
Graphics:	Metallic White	**Dealer:**	Mountain View Chevrolet, Chattanooga, TN
Engine:	427		
Transmission:	Powerglide		

SERIAL NO. 13

Body Style:	Coupe	**Build Own Engine Package:**	No
Color:	Ashen Gray Metallic	**Collectors' Package Engines:**	No
Graphics:	Chevy Racing Blue	**Dealer:**	Bryan Chevrolet, Kenner, LA
Engine:	427		
Transmission:	Powerglide		

SERIAL NO. 14

Body Style:	Coupe	**Build Own Engine Package:**	Yes
Color:	Victory Red	**Collectors' Package Engines:**	427, 327/2.9 SC
Graphics:	Flat Black	**Dealer:**	Pop's Chevrolet, Prestonsburg, KY
Engine:	327/4.0 SC		
Transmission:	Powerglide		

SERIAL NO. 15

Body Style:	Coupe	**Build Own Engine Package:**	No
Color:	Summit White	**Collectors' Package Engines:**	No
Graphics:	Chevy Racing Blue	**Dealer:**	Rockenbach Chevrolet, Grayslake, IL
Engine:	327/4.0 SC		
Transmission:	Powerglide		

SERIAL NO. 16

Body Style:	Coupe
Color:	Black
Graphics:	Inferno Orange
Engine:	427
Transmission:	Powerglide
Build Own Engine Package:	No
Collectors' Package Engines:	327/2.9 SC, 327/4.0 SC
Owner:	Matt Edmiston
Dealer:	The Chevrolet Exchange, Lake Bluff, IL

SERIAL NO. 17

Body Style:	Coupe
Color:	Summit White
Graphics:	Chevy Racing Blue
Engine:	427
Transmission:	Powerglide
Build Own Engine Package:	No
Collectors' Package Engines:	No
Dealer:	Henry Brown Chevrolet, Casa Grande, AZ

SERIAL NO. 18

Body Style:	Coupe
Color:	Summit White
Graphics:	Flat Black
Engine:	427
Transmission:	Powerglide
Build Own Engine Package:	No
Collectors' Package Engines:	No
Dealer:	Ron Tonkin Chevrolet, Portland, OR

SERIAL NO. 19

Body Style:	Coupe
Color:	Victory Red
Graphics:	Flat Black
Engine:	327/4.0 SC
Transmission:	Powerglide
Build Own Engine Package:	No
Collectors' Package Engines:	No
Dealer:	Karl Chevrolet, Ankeny, IA

SERIAL NO. 20

Body Style:	Coupe
Color:	Summit White
Graphics:	Flat Black
Engine:	327/2.9 SC
Transmission:	Powerglide
Build Own Engine Package:	No
Collectors' Package Engines:	No
Dealer:	Friendly Chevrolet, Dallas, TX

SERIAL NO. 21

Body Style:	Coupe
Color:	Summit White
Graphics:	Chevy Racing Blue
Engine:	427
Transmission:	Powerglide
Build Own Engine Package:	Yes
Collectors' Package Engines:	No
Dealer:	Karl Chevrolet, Ankeny, IA

SERIAL NO. 22

Body Style:	Coupe	**Build Own Engine Package:**	No
Color:	Black	**Collectors' Package Engines:**	No
Graphics:	Inferno Orange	**Dealer:**	Scoggin-Dickey Chevrolet, Lubbock, TX
Engine:	427		
Transmission:	Powerglide		

SERIAL NO. 23

Body Style:	Coupe	**Build Own Engine Package:**	Yes
Color:	Victory Red	**Collectors' Package Engines:**	No
Graphics:	Metallic White	**Dealer:**	Bergstrom Chevrolet, Neenah, WI
Engine:	327/4.0 SC		
Transmission:	Powerglide		

SERIAL NO. 24

Body Style:	Coupe
Color:	Victory Red
Graphics:	Flat Black
Engine:	327/2.9 SC
Transmission:	Powerglide
Build Own Engine Package:	Yes
Collectors' Package Engines:	No
Dealer:	Kendall Chevrolet, Eugene, OR

SERIAL NO. 25

Body Style:	Coupe
Color:	Victory Red
Graphics:	No
Engine:	427
Transmission:	Powerglide
Build Own Engine Package:	Yes
Collectors' Package Engines:	No
Dealer:	Courtesy Chevrolet, Phoenix, AZ

SERIAL NO. 26

Body Style:	Coupe
Color:	Summit White
Graphics:	No
Engine:	427
Transmission:	Powerglide
Build Own Engine Package:	Yes
Collectors' Package Engines:	No
Dealer:	Dave Hallman Chevrolet, Erie, PA

SERIAL NO. 27

Body Style:	Coupe
Color:	Black
Graphics:	Flat Black
Engine:	327/4.0 SC
Transmission:	Powerglide
Build Own Engine Package:	No
Collectors' Package Engines:	No
Dealer:	Harchelroad Chevrolet, Imperial, NE

SERIAL NO. 28

Body Style:	Coupe
Color:	Summit White
Graphics:	Inferno Orange
Engine:	427
Transmission:	Powerglide
Build Own Engine Package:	No
Collectors' Package Engines:	No
Dealer:	Porter Chevrolet, Newark, DE

SERIAL NO. 29

Body Style:	Coupe
Color:	Summit White
Graphics:	Chevy Racing Blue
Engine:	427
Transmission:	Powerglide
Build Own Engine Package:	No
Collectors' Package Engines:	No
Dealer:	Mac Haik Chevrolet, Houston, TX

SERIAL NO. 30

Body Style:	Coupe	**Build Own Engine Package:**	No
Color:	Black	**Collectors' Package Engines:**	No
Graphics:	Chevy Racing Blue	**Dealer:**	Ed Bozarth Chevrolet, Grand Junction, CO
Engine:	427		
Transmission:	Powerglide		

SERIAL NO. 31

Body Style:	Coupe	**Build Own Engine Package:**	No
Color:	Black	**Collectors' Package Engines:**	No
Graphics:	Inferno Orange	**Dealer:**	Brian Harris Chevrolet, Baton Rouge, LA
Engine:	327/4.0 SC		
Transmission:	Powerglide		

SERIAL NO. 32

Body Style:	Coupe	**Build Own Engine Package:**	No
Color:	Black	**Collectors' Package Engines:**	No
Graphics:	Chevy Racing Blue	**Dealer:**	Village Chevrolet, Wayzata, MN
Engine:	427		
Transmission:	Powerglide		

SERIAL NO. 33

Body Style:	Coupe	**Build Own Engine Package:**	No
Color:	Black	**Collectors' Package Engines:**	No
Graphics:	Inferno Orange	**Dealer:**	Purifoy Chevrolet, Ft. Lupton, CO
Engine:	427		
Transmission:	Powerglide		

SERIAL NO. 34

Body Style:	Coupe
Color:	Summit White
Graphics:	Chevy Racing Blue
Engine:	427
Transmission:	Powerglide
Build Own Engine Package:	No
Collectors' Package Engines:	No
Dealer:	Paddock Chevrolet, Tonawanda, NY

SERIAL NO. 35

Body Style:	Coupe
Color:	Black
Graphics:	No
Engine:	427
Transmission:	Powerglide
Build Own Engine Package:	No
Collectors' Package Engines:	No
Dealer:	Sewell Chevrolet, Andrews, TX

SERIAL NO. 36

Body Style:	Coupe
Color:	Summit White
Graphics:	Inferno Orange
Engine:	427
Transmission:	Powerglide
Build Own Engine Package:	No
Collectors' Package Engines:	No
Dealer:	Knippelmier Chevrolet, Blanchard, OK

SERIAL NO. 37

Body Style:	Coupe
Color:	Summit White
Graphics:	Chevy Racing Blue
Engine:	327/4.0 SC
Transmission:	Powerglide
Build Own Engine Package:	No
Collectors' Package Engines:	No
Dealer:	Serpentini Chevrolet, Strongsville, OH

SERIAL NO. 38

Body Style:	Coupe
Color:	Silver Ice Metallic
Graphics:	Flat Black
Engine:	427
Transmission:	Powerglide
Build Own Engine Package:	No
Collectors' Package Engines:	No
Dealer:	Don Hattan Chevrolet, Wichita, KS

SERIAL NO. 39

Body Style:	Coupe
Color:	Victory Red
Graphics:	No
Engine:	327/4.0 SC
Transmission:	Powerglide
Build Own Engine Package:	No
Collectors' Package Engines:	No
Dealer:	Edd Kirby's Adventure Chevrolet, Dalton, GA

SERIAL NO. 40

Body Style:	Coupe
Color:	Summit White
Graphics:	Inferno Orange
Engine:	427
Transmission:	Powerglide
Build Own Engine Package:	No
Collectors' Package Engines:	No
Dealer:	Jim Ellis Chevrolet, Atlanta, GA

SERIAL NO. 41

Body Style:	Coupe
Color:	Summit White
Graphics:	Chevy Racing Blue
Engine:	327/4.0 SC
Transmission:	Powerglide
Build Own Engine Package:	No
Collectors' Package Engines:	No
Dealer:	Friendly Chevrolet, Fridley, MN

SERIAL NO. 42

Body Style:	Coupe
Color:	Black
Graphics:	No
Engine:	427
Transmission:	Powerglide
Build Own Engine Package:	No
Collectors' Package Engines:	327/2.9 SC, 327/4.0 SC
Dealer:	George Matick Chevrolet, Redford, MI

SERIAL NO. 43

Body Style:	Coupe
Color:	Summit White
Graphics:	Chevy Racing Blue
Engine:	327/4.0 SC
Transmission:	Powerglide
Build Own Engine Package:	No
Collectors' Package Engines:	No
Dealer:	Mike Savoie Chevrolet, Troy, MI

SERIAL NO. 44

Body Style:	Coupe
Color:	Victory Red
Graphics:	Metallic White
Engine:	427
Transmission:	Powerglide
Build Own Engine Package:	No
Collectors' Package Engines:	No
Dealer:	Murdock Chevrolet, Manhattan, KS

SERIAL NO. 45

Body Style:	Coupe
Color:	Silver Ice Metallic
Graphics:	Flat Black
Engine:	427
Transmission:	Powerglide
Build Own Engine Package:	No
Collectors' Package Engines:	No
Dealer:	Beck Chevrolet, Yonkers, NY

SERIAL NO. 46

Body Style:	Coupe
Color:	Summit White
Graphics:	No
Engine:	427
Transmission:	Powerglide
Build Own Engine Package:	Yes
Collectors' Package Engines:	No
Dealer:	Jim Crivelli Chevrolet, McKees Rocks, PA

SERIAL NO. 47

Body Style:	Coupe
Color:	Black
Graphics:	Flat Black
Engine:	427
Transmission:	Powerglide
Build Own Engine Package:	Yes
Collectors' Package Engines:	No
Owner:	Sam Pierce
Dealer:	Sam Pierce Chevrolet, Daleville, IN

SERIAL NO. 48

Body Style:	Coupe	**Build Own Engine Package:**	No
Color:	Black	**Collectors' Package Engines:**	No
Graphics:	Flat Black	**Dealer:**	Barry's Chevrolet, West Union, OH
Engine:	327/2.9 SC		
Transmission:	Powerglide		

SERIAL NO. 49

Body Style:	Coupe	**Build Own Engine Package:**	No
Color:	Summit White	**Collectors' Package Engines:**	327/2.9 SC, 327/4.0 SC
Graphics:	Chevy Racing Blue	**Dealer:**	Crossroads Chevrolet, Reed City, MI
Engine:	427		
Transmission:	Powerglide		

SERIAL NO. 50

Body Style:	Coupe
Color:	Summit White
Graphics:	Chevy Racing Blue
Engine:	427
Transmission:	Powerglide
Build Own Engine Package:	No
Collectors' Package Engines:	No
Dealer:	Gordon Chevrolet, Tampa, FL

SERIAL NO. 51

Body Style:	Coupe
Color:	Black
Graphics:	Flat Black
Engine:	327/2.9 SC
Transmission:	Powerglide
Build Own Engine Package:	Yes
Collectors' Package Engines:	427, 327/4.0 SC
Dealer:	Sam Pierce Chevrolet, Daleville, IN

SERIAL NO. 52

Body Style:	Coupe
Color:	Black
Graphics:	Metallic White
Engine:	427
Transmission:	Powerglide
Build Own Engine Package:	No
Collectors' Package Engines:	No
Dealer:	Cache River Chevrolet, Ullin, IL

SERIAL NO. 53

Body Style:	Coupe
Color:	Victory Red
Graphics:	No
Engine:	427
Transmission:	Powerglide
Build Own Engine Package:	Yes
Collectors' Package Engines:	No
Dealer:	Dave Hallman Chevrolet, Erie, PA

SERIAL NO. 54

Body Style:	Coupe	**Build Own Engine Package:**	No
Color:	Summit White	**Collectors' Package Engines:**	No
Graphics:	Chevy Racing Blue	**Dealer:**	Stadium Chevrolet, Salem, OH
Engine:	427		
Transmission:	Powerglide		

SERIAL NO. 55

Body Style:	Coupe	**Build Own Engine Package:**	Yes
Color:	Ashen Gray Metallic	**Collectors' Package Engines:**	No
Graphics:	Chevy Racing Blue	**Dealer:**	Carl Black Chevrolet, Kennesaw, GA
Engine:	327/4.0 SC		
Transmission:	Powerglide		

SERIAL NO. 56

Body Style:	Coupe	**Build Own Engine Package:**	No
Color:	Summit White	**Collectors' Package Engines:**	No
Graphics:	Chevy Racing Blue	**Dealer:**	Parks Chevrolet, Augusta, KS
Engine:	427		
Transmission:	Powerglide		

SERIAL NO. 57

Body Style:	Coupe	**Build Own Engine Package:**	No
Color:	Black	**Collectors' Package Engines:**	No
Graphics:	Chevy Racing Blue	**Dealer:**	Greenwood Chevrolet, Austintown, OH
Engine:	327/4.0 SC		
Transmission:	Powerglide		

SERIAL NO. 58

Body Style:	Coupe
Color:	Summit White
Graphics:	Flat Black
Engine:	327/4.0 SC
Transmission:	Powerglide
Build Own Engine Package:	No
Collectors' Package Engines:	No
Dealer:	Bill Stasek Chevrolet, Wheeling, IL

SERIAL NO. 59

Body Style:	Coupe
Color:	Summit White
Graphics:	No
Engine:	427
Transmission:	Powerglide
Build Own Engine Package:	No
Collectors' Package Engines:	No
Dealer:	Taylor Chevrolet, Taylor, MI

SERIAL NO. 60

Body Style:	Coupe
Color:	Summit White
Graphics:	Chevy Racing Blue
Engine:	427
Transmission:	Powerglide
Build Own Engine Package:	No
Collectors' Package Engines:	No
Dealer:	Dobrinsky Chevrolet, Kingfisher, OK

SERIAL NO. 61

Body Style:	Coupe
Color:	Summit White
Graphics:	Chevy Racing Blue
Engine:	427
Transmission:	Powerglide
Build Own Engine Package:	No
Collectors' Package Engines:	No
Dealer:	Robert Chevrolet, Hicksville, NY

SERIAL NO. 62

Body Style:	Coupe
Color:	Victory Red
Graphics:	No
Engine:	427
Transmission:	Powerglide
Build Own Engine Package:	No
Collectors' Package Engines:	No
Dealer:	Chevy 21, Bethlehem, PA

SERIAL NO. 63

Body Style:	Coupe
Color:	Black
Graphics:	No
Engine:	427
Transmission:	Powerglide
Build Own Engine Package:	No
Collectors' Package Engines:	No
Dealer:	Courtesy Chevrolet, Phoenix, AZ

SERIAL NO. 64

Body Style:	Coupe	**Build Own Engine Package:**	No
Color:	Black	**Collectors' Package Engines:**	No
Graphics:	Chevy Racing Blue	**Dealer:**	Team Chevrolet, Salisbury, NC
Engine:	427		
Transmission:	Powerglide		

SERIAL NO. 65

Body Style:	Coupe	**Build Own Engine Package:**	No
Color:	Victory Red	**Collectors' Package Engines:**	No
Graphics:	Flat Black	**Dealer:**	Pogue Chevrolet, Central City, KY
Engine:	327/2.9 SC		
Transmission:	Powerglide		

SERIAL NO. 66

Body Style:	Coupe
Color:	Black
Graphics:	Flat Black
Engine:	427
Transmission:	Powerglide
Build Own Engine Package:	Yes
Collectors' Package Engines:	No
Dealer:	Lofton Chevrolet, Henderson, TN

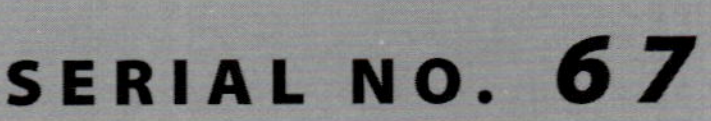

SERIAL NO. 67

Body Style:	Coupe
Color:	Summit White
Graphics:	Chevy Racing Blue
Engine:	427
Transmission:	Powerglide
Build Own Engine Package:	No
Collectors' Package Engines:	No
Dealer:	Paradise Chevrolet, Ventura, CA

SERIAL NO. 68

Body Style:	Convertible
Color:	Black
Graphics:	Metallic White
Engine:	327/4.0 SC
Transmission:	5-speed Manual
Build Own Engine Package:	No
Collectors' Package Engines:	No
Owner:	Chevrolet
Dealer:	None

SERIAL NO. 69

Body Style:	Convertible
Color:	Inferno Orange (custom color)
Graphics:	Carbon Flash, Dark Tarnish Silver
Engine:	327/4.0 SC
Transmission:	3-Speed Automatic
Build Own Engine Package:	No
Collectors' Package Engines:	No

Auctioned for charity: Barrett-Jackson, January 2013

SSA/A 1922

CHAPTER TEN: **COPO AT SPEED**

"Seeing the cars at the strip at the NHRA Nationals was the culmination of the entire COPO project. To finally see a COPO Camaro at the starting line opposite a Cobra Jet Mustang is truly gratifying."

Roger Allen, COPO Camaro Build Manager

Facing page:
The beautiful black COPO Camaro owned and driven by Paul Cambria launches at the starting line of the NHRA U.S. Nationals.

This page: Owner Victor Cagnazzi pays tribute to the late drag racing legend Bill Jenkins with the newest "Grumpy's Toy."

The 2012 NHRA U.S. Nationals were held in Indianapolis on Labor Day weekend. And the COPO Camaro was there. Not just one, but six of them. The spectators were clearly interested in the cars that they had been reading so much about. Even the track announcer, whenever a COPO Camaro approached the starting grid would say something like, "And ladies and gentlemen, we now have one of the new COPO Camaros at the line!" The COPO Camaro was generating the kind of buzz the Chevrolet Performance team had hoped for.

The six COPO Camaros had been in their owners' respective hands for only a few weeks -- in some cases, only a few days. Modifications to the cars were based on the whims, the capabilities and the strategies of the owners, but within NHRA regulations for each class, ranging from significant to none. But the cars were unmistakably COPO Camaros.

As the NHRA Nationals got underway, Cagnazzi

5250
CC/SA
TODD PATTERSON
NHRA
HUSKY
LINERS
VEHICLE PROTECTION THAT LASTS A LIFETIME
Patterson
Racing
Hoosier
JESEL
ARP
Holley
OPTIMA
BATTERIES
SIMPSON
JEGS
Summit
COMPUTECH
MSD
KYMCO
COPO

Facing page: The Patterson Racing/Husky Liners COPO Camaro during an early run at the NHRA U.S. Nationals.

This page: The Patterson Racing COPO in the pits prior to its first qualifying race.

Privateer racer Jim Boburka's Victory Red COPO Camaro, with little ornamentation or modification, exemplifies the factory-built drag car.

Racing's "Grumpy's Toy" COPO Camaro (serial no. 5) won the CC/SA class with Dave Connolly behind the wheel. Connolly's best qualifying time of the weekend was 9.656 seconds for the quarter mile. "This car is fantastic! We only put four runs on it before bringing it here. This is truly a factory-built race car," explains owner Victor Cagnazzi. "We're not here to play, we're here to win."

"I love it!" adds driver Connolly. "I drive a lot of cars and this car is very smooth. The brakes are awesome, it's easy to tune and exhibits both performance and consistency. Chevy definitely did their homework with this car. It's right up there on the 'fun meter.'"

A class win against competitors that have had years to set up and tune their entries was very impressive. It serves as testament to the skills and determination of the Chevrolet Performance team to deliver a Camaro worthy of the COPO's winning heritage right out of the box.

Also competing in the CC/SA class was Todd Patterson, driving the Husky Liners COPO Camaro (serial no. 18), posting a qualifying time of 9.534 seconds. Patterson Racing's Allan Patterson, Todd, and car owner Bob Tyler had taken delivery of their COPO Camaro at the Chevrolet Performance Build Center just two weeks before on August 17, 2012. They immediately took the car to Topeka for testing and to prepare it for the NHRA U.S. Nationals in Indianapolis.

Competing in the BB/SA class was Eric Reyes, driving the Jimmy Vasser Chevrolet COPO Camaro (serial no. 4). "I've been racing cars a long time, and this is the first time I've driven anything with a blower [supercharger]." It's really smooth on the track and the acceleration is incredible. It just keeps pulling, pulling, pulling. The very first time we had it on the track, we did 9.38 and about 149 miles per hour. Just incredible." At Indianapolis, Reyes posted a qualifying time of 9.543 seconds.

Competing in the BB/SA class as well was privateer and Chevy dealer Jim Boburka Sr., notably driving the only red COPO Camaro (serial no. 7) seen at Indianapolis and posting a respectable 9.624 seconds for the quarter mile. Boburka's COPO was literally unchanged from when he burned rubber driving it out of the Perfor-

Cagnazzi Racing's "Grumpy's Toy" won the CC/SA class with Dave Connolly driving.

mance Build Center on August 8, 2012, except for a new front grill from the Chevy Performance Parts catalog. Boburka has been drag racing since 1965, and formerly raced a 1969 Camaro ZL1 that never saw the street.

"Since 2008, I've been telling anyone at GM who would listen," recalls Boburka. "I'd say, 'We Chevy people need something to compete with!' I e-mailed everyone I knew at GM. I even called [GM President of North America] Mark Reuss. Within ten minutes he called me back, simply saying 'just be patient.' So that's what I did. I waited, and I'm fortunate to finally own one. This car has exceeded my expectations. It's over the top!"

Another privateer racer at Indianapolis was Paul

Above: The ATI COPO Camaro, owned by J.C. Beattie Jr., was the most modified COPO at the U.S. Nationals, yet remained an unmistakable COPO.

Below: This was the sight everyone had looked forward to: a COPO Camaro going head-to-head with a Cobra Jet Mustang.

Below left: Paul Cambria was one of several COPO owners to install a drag chute.

Above and below right: Jimmy Vasser driver Eric Reyes was responsible for the eye-catching graphics on their "King Kong Copo."

These pages: The COPO Camaros undoubtedly were the talk of the sportsmen classes at the 2012 NHRA U.S. Nationals. They presented well and ran very fast.

Cambria, competing in the SSA/A class driving his black COPO Camaro (serial no. 3), posting a very fast elapsed qualifying time of 8.718 seconds. Cambria will forever be known as the first customer to take delivery of a 2012 COPO Camaro from the Performance Build Center, driving it out of the facility shortly after noon on August 8.

"Racing is a hobby for me," explains Cambria. "I'm a Chevy guy, but my friends were buying Mustangs, and since Chevrolet had no offering, I ordered a Cobra Jet as well. When I went to the SEMA Show in 2011, and learned that Chevy was going to build the COPO Camaro, I expressed great interest. When I finally got the call telling me I had been selected to buy one, I wired my Chevy dealer the money in 15 minutes. I didn't want them changing their minds! The next thing I did was to notify the Ford dealer that I was canceling my Cobra Jet order. The dealer wasn't surprised. He said, 'I know, I know. A Camaro, right?'" Cambria even coined his

own motto, in reference to his jet black COPO Camaro: "Black over blue, the CJs are through!"

Another competitor in the SSA/A class was J.C. Beattie's ATI-sponsored COPO Camaro (serial no. 8) driven by Marty Rinehart Jr. This was the most heavily modified COPO at Indianapolis and posted a speedy qualifying time of 8.667 seconds for the quarter mile.

Every one of the six COPO Camaros posted respectable times, with very little time for setup. It was a great debut for the cars the team had worked so hard on for several years. The Performance Team never lost sight of the ultimate goal for the COPO Camaro: the drag strip.

"Seeing the cars at the strip at the NHRA Nationals was the culmination of the entire COPO project," says COPO Build Manager Roger Allen. "It was a process that included a lot of input from a lot of people, from conception to customer delivery. To finally see a COPO Camaro at the starting line opposite a Cobra Jet Mustang is truly gratifying."

Perhaps no one summed up the excitement better that Jimmy Vasser driver Reyes: "I'm proud to be a part of history. I'm proud to be a part of the comeback of the Bowtie in grassroots drag racing."

APPENDIX ONE: **2012 COPO CAMARO SPECIFICATIONS**

GENERAL INFORMATION

NHRA horsepower ratings

327 cu. in. / 4.0L supercharged – 550 hp
327 cu. in. / 2.9L supercharged – 500 hp
427 cu. in. / naturally aspirated – 425 hp

NHRA shipping weights

327 cu. in. / 4.0L supercharged – 3175 lbs.
327 cu. in. / 2.9L supercharged – 3250 lbs.
427 cu. in. / naturally aspirated – 3195 lbs.

Specifications for 3-speed auto and manual transmissions submitted to NHRA for use in Stock and Super Stock classes

Recommended max engine rpm – 7500

CHASSIS

Chromoly cage – NHRA certified to 8.50 ET

Sub-frames tied together

Front engine cradle modified to accept additional oil pan clearance

Rear sub-frame modified to accept unique COPO NHRA Stock Eliminator suspension

REAR SUSPENSION

4-bar with adjustable top links

Adjustable Panhard link

Double-adjustable Strange Engineering coil-over shocks

Anti-roll bar

FRONT SUSPENSION

Adjustable Strange Engineering coil-over struts

Sway bar removed

STEERING

Production steering gear modified for manual (non-assist) operation

BRAKES

Lightweight vented rotors

Billet four-piston light-weight calipers

Lightweight tandem master cylinder

OEM pedal modified to mount master cylinder

All components provided by Strange Engineering

WHEELS

Bogart Racing lightweight with unique COPO logo

Forged outer ring

Billet center

15 in. x 10 in. rear – 5/8 in. studs

15 in. x 3.5 in. front – 1/2 in. studs

4 3/4 in. bolt circle pattern

TIRES

Rear – 9.0 / 30.0R - 15 94.0 in. radial

Front – 4.5 / 28.0 – 15 in. drag only

GEARS & AXLES

Strange Engineering 9 in. aluminum center section

Lightweight steel spool

Strange Engineering 9310 alloy 4.29:1 ring & pinion set for 427 and 327 2.9L SC, 4.10:1 for 327 4.0L SC

Strange Engineering 35-spline axles

Strange Engineering chromoly yoke

DRIVE SHAFT

4 in. OD x .125 in. wall 6061-T6 aluminum tube

Chromoly end caps

Forged chromoly slip yoke

Heavy-duty 1350 universal joints

TRANSMISSION

ATI Racing Products "Pro Glide"

- SFI-approved ATI "Super Case"
- 1.80 ratio 9310 straight-cut gear set
- Precision balanced carrier with 4340 tool steel output shaft
- Turbo spline input shaft:
  - 327 / 4.0L – Vasco material
  - 327 / 2.9L and 427 – 300M material
- Seven-clutch high gear pack
- Billet clutch hub
- High-flow front pump with heat-treated pinned stator tube
- Deep aluminum pan
- Hard chrome Rings
- Fluid overflow catch can

TORQUE CONVERTER

(unique for each application)

ATI Racing Products "Treemaster MRT" Series

- 327 / 4.0L – 9 in. diameter housing
  - Furnace brazed impeller and turbine fins
  - Precision pump drive tube
  - Heavy duty needle bearings
  - 22 element sprag with dual cage construction
- 327 / 2.9L and 427 – 8 in. diameter housing
  - Furnace brazed impeller and turbine fins
  - Precision pump drive tube
  - Heavy duty needle bearings
  - Investment cast cover

SHIFTER

Hurst "Quarter Stick" – 2-speed automatic

- Forward pattern
- Built-in neutral safety switch
- Lightweight aluminum cover

327 ENGINE

Chevrolet Performance "LSX" cast iron block with steel main caps

4.065 in. bore x 3.150 in. stroke

Static compression ratio – 10:1 nominal

Callies 4340 crankshaft – double-keyed snout

Callies 4340 H-beam "Ultra" rods

- 6.350 in. c-c length
- .928 in. pin bore diameter

Clevite H-Series heat-treated tri-metal rod & main bearings

Mahle 2618 alloy forged domed pistons

- Grafal coating
- Hard-anodized top ring groove
- Friction-coated skirts

Mahle .043 in. x .043 in. x 3mm piston rings

- Ductile iron top with radius molybdenum face
- Plain cast iron tapered 2nd
- Chrome-plated oil rails with low-tension expander

Comp Cams steel billet hydraulic roller camshaft

- Duration – 246° IN / 254° EX @ .050" lift
- Theoretical valve lift - .630" IN / .630" EX
- Lobe centers – 117°

APPENDIX ONE: 2012 COPOCAMARO SPECIFICATIONS (continued)

Valvetrain
- Chevrolet Performance "Ceramic Ball" high-rpm hydraulic roller tappets
- 3/8 in. diameter LS7 pushrods
- 1.8:1 ratio LS7 rocker arms with roller trunnions
- PSI "Max Life" beehive valve springs
- Hardened-steel spring seats
- Lightweight steel retainers

Fully CNC'd aluminum cylinder heads – based on LS7
- 275 cc nominal intake port volume
- 89 cc nominal exhaust port volume
- 70 cc nominal combustion chamber volume
- Del West titanium intake valves – 2.205 in. head dia. x 7mm stem
- Lightweight sodium-filled exhaust valves – 1.615 in. head dia. x 7mm stem

Fel-Pro Performance multi-layer steel head gaskets with raised cylinder sealing bead

Internal wet sump oil pump

Deep-sump cast aluminum oil pan – 6-quart capacity

ATI Performance Products SFI-approved damper – 10-rib shell

Whipple twin-screw supercharger
- 327 cu.in. / 550 hp – 4.0L
- 327 cu.in. / 500 hp – 2.9L

Whipple billet throttle body
- 327 cu.in. / 550 hp – 172mm oval blade
- 327 cu.in. / 500 hp – 109mm round blade

Headers
- 2 in. x 30 in. primary with 30 in. merge collectors
- 304 stainless steel

427 ENGINE

Chevrolet Performance LS7 aluminum block

4.125 in. bore x 4.00 in. stroke

Static compression ratio – 13:1 nominal

Callies 5140 crankshaft

Callies 4340 H-beam rods
- 6.100 in. c-c length
- .928 in. pin bore diameter

Clevite H-Series heat-treated TriMetal rod & main bearings

Mahle 2618 alloy forged domed pistons
- Grafal coating
- Hard-anodized top ring groove
- Friction-coated skirts

Mahle .043 in. x .043 in. x 3mm piston rings
- Ductile iron top with radius molybdenum face
- Plain cast iron tapered 2nd
- Chrome-plated oil rails with low-tension expander

Chevrolet Performance steel billet hydraulic roller camshaft
- Duration – 233° IN / 276° EX @ .050" lift
- Theoretical valve lift - .630" IN / .630" EX
- Lobe centers – 107°

Valvetrain
- Chevrolet Performance "Ceramic Ball" high-RPM hy draulic roller tappets
- 3/8 in. diameter LS7 pushrods
- 1.8:1 ratio LS7 rocker arms with roller trunnions
- PSI "Max Life" beehive valve springs
- Hardened steel spring seats
- Light-weight steel retainers

Fully CNC'd aluminum cylinder heads – based on LS7
- 275cc nominal intake port volume
- 89cc nominal exhaust port volume
- 70cc nominal combustion chamber volume
- Del West titanium intake valves – 2.205 in. head dia. x 7mm stem
- Light-weight sodium-filled exhaust valves – 1.615 in. head dia. x 7mm stem

Fel-Pro Performance multi-layer steel head gaskets with raised cylinder sealing bead

Internal wet sump oil pump

Deep-sump cast aluminum oil pan – 6-quart capacity

ATI Performance Products SFI-approved damper

Meziere billet electric water pump

Chevrolet Performance / Holley "Hi Ram" intake manifold

Whipple billet throttle body – 102mm blade

Headers
- 2 in. x 30 in. primary with 30 in. merge collectors
- 304 stainless steel

FUEL SYSTEM

Aeromotive "Eliminator" fuel pump - free flow rating = 800 lb/hr

Aeromotive A1000 pressure regulator with manifold pressure compensation capability

Aeromotive 10-micron high-flow filter

Light-weight black nylon braided -8 AN hoses

Black anodized aluminum -8 AN hose ends and fittings

Fuel Pressure:
- 327 - 70 psi base (1 to 1 boost compsensation used for supercharged engines)
- 427 - 90 psi base High-impedance fuel injectors
- 327 cu.in. / 550 hp – 105 lb/hr @ 43.5 psi with EV1 connector
- 327 cu.in. / 500 hp – 80 lb/hr @ 43.5 psi with EV1 connector
- 427 cu.in. / 425 hp – 42 lb/hr @ 58 psi with EV6 / USCAR connector

ENGINE CONTROLS & IGNITION

Delco MEFI 5A electronic fuel injection processor
- Speed density operation
- Interfacing software and hardware available in the aftermarket

Cable-actuated throttle

Production LS7 ignition coils

Production LS7 secondary wires

GM sensors

ELECTRICAL

Dash-installed control switches
- Starter
- Ignition
- Fuel pump
- Cooling fan
- Intercooler pump/water pump, depending on engine package

GAUGES

Autometer with gold "Bowtie" logo on dials
- 5 in. 10,000 rpm tach with shift light
- Electronic water temp with 2 1/16 in. face and 100°- 260°F range
- Electronic trans temp with 2 1/16 in. face and 100°- 260°F range
- Electronic oil pressure with 2 1/16 in. face and 0 - 100 psi range
- Electronic fuel pressure with 2 1/16 in. face and 0 - 100 psi range
- Voltmeter with 2 1/16 in. face and 8 - 18v range

SAFETY

RJS Safety Equipment 3 in. driver restraints

RJS Safety Equipment window net

APPENDIX TWO: **CAMARO GENERATIONS**

FIRST GENERATION

1967

Trim Levels:
Base, RS, SS, Z28

GM Platform:
F-body

Engines:

230 cu.in.	6	140 hp	1-bbl
250 cu.in.	6	155 hp	1-bbl
327 cu.in.	V8	210 hp	2-bbl
327 cu.in.	V8	275 hp	4-bbl
350 cu.in.	V8	295 hp	4-bbl

Transmission:
3-speed manual
4-speed manual
Powerglide automatic

Wheelbase: 108 in.

Final Assembly:
Norwood, Ohio
Van Nuys, California

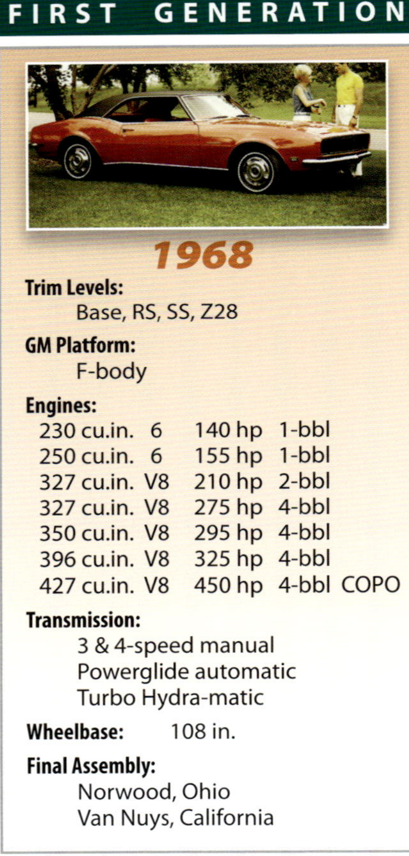

1968

Trim Levels:
Base, RS, SS, Z28

GM Platform:
F-body

Engines:

230 cu.in.	6	140 hp	1-bbl	
250 cu.in.	6	155 hp	1-bbl	
327 cu.in.	V8	210 hp	2-bbl	
327 cu.in.	V8	275 hp	4-bbl	
350 cu.in.	V8	295 hp	4-bbl	
396 cu.in.	V8	325 hp	4-bbl	
427 cu.in.	V8	450 hp	4-bbl	COPO

Transmission:
3 & 4-speed manual
Powerglide automatic
Turbo Hydra-matic

Wheelbase: 108 in.

Final Assembly:
Norwood, Ohio
Van Nuys, California

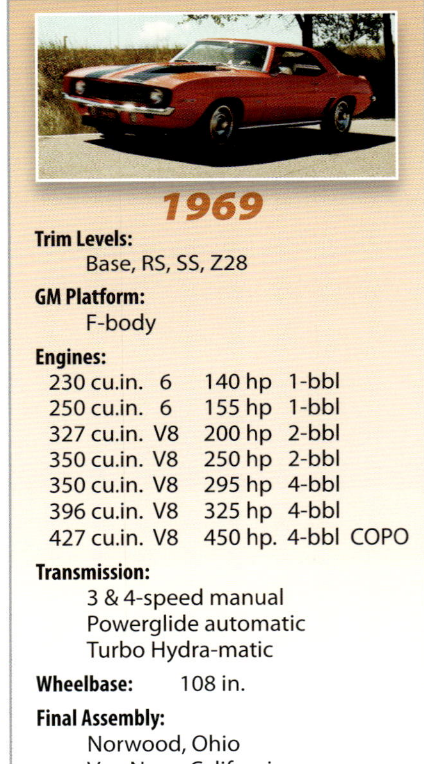

1969

Trim Levels:
Base, RS, SS, Z28

GM Platform:
F-body

Engines:

230 cu.in.	6	140 hp	1-bbl	
250 cu.in.	6	155 hp	1-bbl	
327 cu.in.	V8	200 hp	2-bbl	
350 cu.in.	V8	250 hp	2-bbl	
350 cu.in.	V8	295 hp	4-bbl	
396 cu.in.	V8	325 hp	4-bbl	
427 cu.in.	V8	450 hp.	4-bbl	COPO

Transmission:
3 & 4-speed manual
Powerglide automatic
Turbo Hydra-matic

Wheelbase: 108 in.

Final Assembly:
Norwood, Ohio
Van Nuys, California

All data obtained from actual product catalogs and may not reflect mid-year or running changes.

1970

Trim Levels:
Camaro, RS, SS, Z28

GM Platform:
F-body

Engines:

250 cu.in.	6	155 hp	1-bbl
307 cu.in.	V8	200 hp	2-bbl
350 cu.in.	V8	250 hp	2-bbl
350 cu.in.	V8	300 hp	4-bbl
350 cu.in.	V8	360 hp	4-bbl
396 cu.in.	V8	350 hp	4-bbl

Transmission:
3-speed manual
4-speed manual
Powerglide automatic
Turbo Hydra-matic

Wheelbase: 108 in.

Final Assembly:
Norwood, Ohio
Van Nuys, California

1971

Trim Levels:
Camaro, RS, SS, Z28

GM Platform:
F-body

Engines:

250 cu.in.	6	155 hp (110)*	1-bbl
307 cu.in.	V8	200 hp (140)*	2-bbl
350 cu.in.	V8	245 hp (165)*	2-bbl
350 cu.in.	V8	270 hp (210)*	4-bbl
350 cu.in.	V8	330 hp (275)*	4-bbl
396 cu.in.	V8	300 hp (260)*	4-bbl

Transmission:
3 & 4-speed manual
Powerglide automatic
Turbo Hydra-matic

Wheelbase: 108 in.

Final Assembly:
Norwood, Ohio
Van Nuys, California

* Horsepower figures in parentheses reflect change to SAE net standard.

1972

Trim Levels:
Camaro, RS, SS, Z28

GM Platform:
F-body

Engines:

250 cu.in.	6	110 hp	1-bbl
307 cu.in.	V8	130 hp	2-bbl
350 cu.in.	V8	165 hp	2-bbl
350 cu.in.	V8	200 hp	4-bbl
350 cu.in.	V8	255 hp	4-bbl
396 cu.in.*	V8	240 hp	4-bbl

Transmission:
3 & 4-speed manual
Powerglide automatic
Turbo Hydra-matic

Wheelbase: 108 in.

Final Assembly:
Norwood, Ohio

* Actual displacement is 402 cu.in..

1973

Trim Levels:
Sport Coupe, Type LT, RS, Z28

GM Platform:
F-body

Engines:

250 cu.in.	6	100 hp	1-bbl
307 cu.in.	V8	115 hp	2-bbl
350 cu.in.	V8	145 hp	2-bbl
350 cu.in.	V8	175 hp	4-bbl
350 cu.in.	V8	245 hp	4-bbl

Transmission:
3-speed manual
4-speed manual
Turbo Hydra-matic

Wheelbase: 108 in.

Final Assembly:
Norwood, Ohio

All data obtained from actual product catalogs and may not reflect mid-year or running changes.

1974

Trim Levels:
Type LT, Z28

GM Platform:
F-body

Engines:

250 cu.in.	6	100 hp	1-bbl
350 cu.in.	V8	145 hp	2-bbl
350 cu.in.	V8	160 hp	4-bbl
350 cu.in.	V8	185 hp	4-bbl
350 cu.in.	V8	245 hp	4-bbl

Transmission:
3-speed manual
4-speed manual
Turbo Hydra-matic

Wheelbase: 108 in.

Final Assembly:
Norwood, Ohio

1975

Trim Levels:
Sport Coupe, Type LT

GM Platform:
F-body

Engines:

250 cu.in.	6	105 hp	1-bbl
350 cu.in.	V8	145 hp	2-bbl
350 cu.in.	V8	155 hp	4-bbl

Transmission:
3-speed manual
4-speed manual
Turbo Hydra-matic

Wheelbase: 108 in.

Final Assembly:
Norwood, Ohio

1976

Trim Levels:
Sport Coupe, Type LT, RS

GM Platform:
F-body

Engines:

250 cu.in.	6	105 hp	1-bbl
350 cu.in.	V8	140 hp	2-bbl
350 cu.in.	V8	165 hp	4-bbl

Transmission:
3-speed manual
4-speed manual
Turbo Hydra-matic

Wheelbase: 108 in.

Final Assembly:
Norwood, Ohio
Van Nuys, California

1977

Trim Levels:
Sport Coupe, Type LT, RS, Z28

GM Platform:
F-body

Engines:

250 cu.in.	6	110 hp	1-bbl
350 cu.in.	V8	145 hp	2-bbl
350 cu.in.	V8	170 hp	4-bbl

Transmission:
3-speed manual
4-speed manual
Turbo Hydra-matic

Wheelbase: 108 in.

Final Assembly:
Norwood, Ohio
Van Nuys, California

SECOND GENERATION (continued)

1978

Trim Levels:
Type LT, RS, Z28

GM Platform:
F-body

Engines:

250 cu.in.	6	110 hp	1-bbl
350 cu.in.	V8	145 hp	2-bbl
350 cu.in.	V8	170 hp	4-bbl

Transmission:
3-speed manual
4-speed manual
3-speed automatic

Wheelbase: 108 in.

Final Assembly:
Norwood, Ohio
Van Nuys, California

1979

Trim Levels:
Sport Coupe, Berlinetta, RS, SS, Z28

GM Platform:
F-body

Engines:

4.1L (250 ci)	6	115 hp	1-bbl
5.0L (305 ci)	V8	145 hp	2-bbl
5.7L (350 ci)	V8	170 hp	4-bbl
5.7L (350 ci)	V8	175 hp	4-bbl

Transmission:
3-speed manual
4-speed manual
3-speed automatic

Wheelbase: 108 in.

Final Assembly:
Norwood, Ohio
Van Nuys, California

1980

Trim Levels:
Sport Coupe, Berlinetta, RS, SS, Z28

GM Platform:
F-body

Engines:

3.8L (229 ci)	V6	115 hp	2-bbl
4.4L (267 ci)	V8	120 hp	2-bbl
5.0L (305 ci)	V8	155 hp	4-bbl
5.7L (350 ci)	V8	190 hp	4-bbl

Transmission:
3-speed manual
4-speed manual
3-speed automatic

Wheelbase: 108 in.

Final Assembly:
Norwood, Ohio
Van Nuys, California

1981

Trim Levels:
Sport Coupe, Berlinetta, Z28

GM Platform:
F-body

Engines:

3.8L (229 ci)	V6	110 hp	2-bbl
4.4L (267 ci)	V8	120 hp	2-bbl
5.0L (305 ci)	V8	145 hp	4-bbl
5.0L (305 ci)	V8	165 hp	4-bbl (Z28)
5.7L (350 ci)	V8	175 hp	4-bbl

Transmission:
3-speed manual
4-speed manual
3-speed automatic

Wheelbase: 108 in.

Final Assembly:
Norwood, Ohio
Van Nuys, California

THIRD GENERATION

1982

Trim Levels:
Sport Coupe, Berlinetta, Z28

GM Platform:
F-body

Engines:

2.5L (151 ci)	4	90 hp	F.I.
2.8L (173 ci)	V6	102 hp	2-bbl
5.0L (305 ci)	V8	145 hp	4-bbl
5.0L (305 ci)	V8	145 hp	F.I.

Transmission:
4-speed manual
3-speed automatic

Wheelbase: 101 in.

Final Assembly:
Norwood, Ohio
Van Nuys, California

1983

Trim Levels:
Sport Coupe, Berlinetta, Z28

GM Platform:
F-body

Engines:

2.5L (151 ci)	4	90 hp	F.I.
2.8L (173 ci)	V6	102 hp	2-bbl
5.0L (305 ci)	V8	145 hp	4-bbl
5.0L (305 ci)	V8	145 hp	F.I.

Transmission:
4-speed manual
5-speed manual
3-speed automatic
4-speed automatic

Wheelbase: 101 in.

Final Assembly:
Norwood, Ohio
Van Nuys, California

1984

Trim Levels:
Sport Coupe, Berlinetta, Z28

GM Platform:
F-body

Engines:

2.5L (151 ci)	4	90 hp	F.I.
2.8L (173 ci)	V6	102 hp	2-bbl
5.0L (305 ci)	V8	145 hp	4-bbl
5.0L (305 ci)	V8	190 hp	4-bbl

Transmission:
4-speed manual
5-speed manual
4-speed automatic

Wheelbase: 101 in.

Final Assembly:
Norwood, Ohio
Van Nuys, California

1985

Trim Levels:
Sport Coupe, Berlinetta, Z28

GM Platform:
F-body

Engines:

2.5L (151 ci)	4	88 hp	F.I.
2.8L (173 ci)	V6	135 hp	F.I.
5.0L (305 ci)	V8	155 hp	4-bbl
5.0L (305 ci)	V8	190 hp	4-bbl
5.0L (305 ci)	V8	215 hp	F.I.

Transmission:
5-speed manual
4-speed automatic

Wheelbase: 101 in.

Final Assembly:
Norwood, Ohio
Van Nuys, California

1986

Trim Levels:
Sport Coupe, Berlinetta, Z28, IROC-Z

GM Platform:
F-body

Engines:

2.5L (151 ci)	4	88 hp	F.I.
2.8L (173 ci)	V6	135 hp	F.I.
5.0L (305 ci)	V8	155 hp	4-bbl
5.0L (305 ci)	V8	190 hp	4-bbl
5.0L (305 ci)	V8	190 hp	F.I.

Transmission:
5-speed manual
4-speed automatic

Wheelbase: 101 in.

Final Assembly:
Norwood, Ohio
Van Nuys, California

1987

Trim Levels:
Sport Coupe, LT, Z28, IROC-Z

GM Platform:
F-body

Engines:

2.8L (173 ci)	V6	135 hp	F.I.
5.0L (305 ci)	V8	170 hp	4-bbl
5.0L (305 ci)	V8	190 hp	F.I.
5.7L (350 ci)	V8	230 hp	F.I.

Transmission:
5-speed manual
4-speed automatic

Wheelbase: 101 in.

Final Assembly:
Norwood, Ohio
Van Nuys, California

1988

Trim Levels:
Sport Coupe, IROC-Z

GM Platform:
F-body

Engines:

2.8L (173 ci)	V6	135 hp	F.I.
5.0L (305 ci)	V8	170 hp	F.I.
5.0L (305 ci)	V8	220 hp	F.I.
5.7L (350 ci)	V8	230 hp	F.I.

Transmission:
5-speed manual
4-speed automatic

Wheelbase: 101 in.

Final Assembly:
Van Nuys, California

1989

Trim Levels:
RS, IROC-Z

GM Platform:
F-body

Engines:

2.8L (173 ci)	V6	135 hp	F.I.
5.0L (305 ci)	V8	230 hp	F.I.
5.7L (350 ci)	V8	240 hp	F.I.

Transmission:
5-speed manual
4-speed automatic

Wheelbase: 101 in.

Final Assembly:
Van Nuys, California

All data obtained from actual product catalogs and may not reflect mid-year or running changes.

1990

Trim Levels:
RS, IROC-Z

GM Platform:
F-body

Engines:

3.1L (191 ci)	V6	140 hp	F.I.
5.0L (305 ci)	V8	230 hp	F.I.
5.7L (350 ci)	V8	240 hp	F.I.

Transmission:
5-speed manual
4-speed automatic

Wheelbase: 101 in.

Final Assembly:
Van Nuys, California

1991

Trim Levels:
RS, Z28

GM Platform:
F-body

Engines:

3.1L (191 ci)	V6	140 hp	F.I.
5.0L (305 ci)	V8	170 hp	F.I.
5.0L (305 ci)	V8	230 hp	F.I.
5.7L (350 ci)	V8	245 hp	F.I.

Transmission:
5-speed manual
4-speed automatic

Wheelbase: 101 in.

Final Assembly:
Van Nuys, California

1992

Trim Levels:
RS, Z28

GM Platform:
F-body

Engines:

3.1L (191 ci)	V6	140 hp	F.I.
5.0L (305 ci)	V8	170 hp	F.I.
5.0L (305 ci)	V8	230 hp	F.I.
5.7L (350 ci)	V8	245 hp	F.I.

Transmission:
5-speed manual
4-speed automatic

Wheelbase: 101 in.

Final Assembly:
Van Nuys, California

FOURTH GENERATION

1993

Trim Levels:
Camaro, Z28

GM Platform:
F-body

Engines:
3.4L V6 160 hp F.I.
5.7L V8 275 hp F.I. LT1

Transmission:
5-speed manual
6-speed manual
4-speed automatic

Wheelbase: 101.1 in.

Final Assembly:
Sainte-Thérèse, Quebec

1994

Trim Levels:
Camaro, Z28

GM Platform:
F-body

Engines:
3.4L V6 160 hp F.I.
5.7L V8 275 hp F.I. LT1

Transmission:
5-speed manual
6-speed manual
4-speed automatic

Wheelbase: 101.1 in.

Final Assembly:
Sainte-Thérèse, Quebec

1995

Trim Levels:
Camaro, Z28

GM Platform:
F-body

Engines:
3.4L V6 160 hp F.I.
3800 V6 200 hp F.I. (Calif. only)
5.7L V8 275 hp F.I. LT1

Transmission:
5-speed manual
6-speed manual
4-speed automatic

Wheelbase: 101.1 in.

Final Assembly:
Sainte-Thérèse, Quebec

1996

Trim Levels:
Camaro, RS, Z28

GM Platform:
F-body

Engines:
3800 V6 200 hp F.I.
5.7L V8 285 hp F.I. LT1

Transmission:
5-speed manual
6-speed manual
4-speed automatic

Wheelbase: 101.1 in.

Final Assembly:
Sainte-Thérèse, Quebec

All data obtained from actual product catalogs and may not reflect mid-year or running changes.

1997

Trim Levels:
Camaro, RS, Z28, 30th Anniv. Ed.

GM Platform:
F-body

Engines:
3800 V6 200 hp F.I.
5.7L V8 285 hp F.I. LT1

Transmission:
5-speed manual
6-speed manual
4-speed automatic

Wheelbase: 101.1 in.

Final Assembly:
Sainte-Thérèse, Quebec

1998

Trim Levels:
Camaro, SS, Z28

GM Platform:
F-body

Engines:
3800 V6 200 hp F.I.
5.7L V8 305 hp F.I. LS1
5.7L V8 320 hp F.I. LS1

Transmission:
5-speed manual
6-speed manual
4-speed automatic

Wheelbase: 101.1 in.

Final Assembly:
Sainte-Thérèse, Quebec

1999

Trim Levels:
Camaro, SS, Z28

GM Platform:
F-body

Engines:
3800 V6 200 hp F.I.
5.7L V8 305 hp F.I. LS1
5.7L V8 320 hp F.I. LS1

Transmission:
5-speed manual
6-speed manual
4-speed automatic

Wheelbase: 101.1 in.

Final Assembly:
Sainte-Thérèse, Quebec

FOURTH GENERATION (continued)

2000

Trim Levels:
Camaro, SS, Z28

GM Platform:
F-body

Engines:
3800 V6 200 hp F.I.
5.7L V8 305 hp F.I. LS1
5.7L V8 320 hp F.I. LS1

Transmission:
5-speed manual
6-speed manual
4-speed automatic

Wheelbase: 101.1 in.

Final Assembly:
Sainte-Thérèse, Quebec

2001

Trim Levels:
Camaro, SS, Z28

GM Platform:
F-body

Engines:
3800 V6 200 hp F.I.
5.7L V8 310 hp F.I. LS1
5.7L V8 325 hp F.I. LS1

Transmission:
5-speed manual
6-speed manual
4-speed automatic

Wheelbase: 101.1 in.

Final Assembly:
Sainte-Thérèse, Quebec

2002

Trim Levels:
Camaro, SS, Z28

GM Platform:
F-body

Engines:
3800 V6 200 hp F.I.
5.7L V8 305 hp F.I. LS1
5.7L V8 320 hp F.I. LS1

Transmission:
5-speed manual
6-speed manual
4-speed automatic

Wheelbase: 101.1 in.

Final Assembly:
Sainte-Thérèse, Quebec

FIFTH GENERATION

2010

Trim Levels:
LS, LT, SS (RS Package)

GM Platform:
Zeta

Engines:
3.6L V6 304 hp F.I.
6.2L V8 400 hp F.I. (automatic)
6.2L V8 426 hp F.I. (manual)

Transmission:
6-speed manual
6-speed automatic

Wheelbase: 112.3 in.

Final Assembly:
Oshawa, Ontario

2011

Trim Levels:
LS, LT, SS (RS Package)

GM Platform:
Zeta

Engines:
3.6L V6 312 hp F.I.
6.2L V8 400 hp F.I. (automatic)
6.2L V8 426 hp F.I. (manual)

Transmission:
6-speed manual
6-speed automatic

Wheelbase: 112.3 in.

Final Assembly:
Oshawa, Ontario

2012

Trim Levels:
LS, LT, SS (RS Package, 45th Anniversary Package), ZL1

GM Platform:
Zeta

Engines:
3.6L V6 323 hp F.I.
6.2L V8 400 hp F.I. (automatic)
6.2L V8 426 hp F.I. (manual)
6.2L V8 580 hp S.C. (ZL1)

Transmission:
6-speed manual
6-speed automatic

Wheelbase: 112.3 in.

Final Assembly:
Oshawa, Ontario

2013

Trim Levels:
LS, LT, SS (RS Package), ZL1

GM Platform:
Zeta

Engines:
3.6L V6 323 hp F.I.
6.2L V8 400 hp F.I. (automatic)
6.2L V8 426 hp F.I. (manual)
6.2L V8 580 hp S.C. (ZL1)

Transmission:
6-speed manual
6-speed automatic

Wheelbase: 112.3 in.

Final Assembly:
Oshawa, Ontario

ACKNOWLEDGEMENTS

"This is a project we'll never forget. Everyone on this team is an enthusiast, so we all understand the importance of continuing the COPO legacy. But this project also adds to the long and proud Chevrolet legacy."

Sandor Piszar, Chevrolet Performance Director

"I'm very fortunate to have been given the opportunity to work on this project."

Robin Wright, COPO Program Manager

"Working on this program has been a privilege. We're creating history while being respectful of the past."

Cliff Cohen, Chevy Performance Marketing Manager

Though these words belong to Sandor Piszar, Robin Wright and Cliff Cohen, they are echoed, to a person, by everyone with whom I interviewed for this book. I, too, feel privileged to have been a part of this project and given total access to the people, processes and products of the Chevy Performance Team. I want to thank everyone for giving me their time and sharing their enthusiasm. This book would not have been possible without their assistance.

I would particularly like to thank Dr. Jamie Meyer, my primary contact on this endeavor. Jamie opened doors for me, established contacts, and provided guidance from start to finish. Jamie holds a Ph.D. in cardiovascular research and had joined GM just a few years before the COPO project was approved. He is now serving as performance marketing manager. The lure of motorsports and high-performance racing were too great to keep him in the medical field. It has been said that if anyone at Chevrolet understands the anatomical bio-mechanics of "heart-pumping" performance, it is the good Dr. Meyer. Thank you, Jamie.

I would also like to thank Chevy Performance Director Sandor Piszar. His enthusiasm for Chevrolet Performance, for Camaro, and for COPO is nothing short of infectious. One needs only to spend a few minutes with Sandor to get an incurable case of "Chevy Fever." His ongoing guidance and suggestions throughout the project were helpful and greatly appreciated. Thank you, Sandor.

I would especially like to thank COPO Project Manager Robin Wright and MPR Race Car's Mike Pustelny for sharing with me the nuts and bolts of building a competitive world-class drag racer. Both spent more time with me than I'm sure they expected to spend. Robin and Mike, please know that your participation was extremely beneficial and is very much appreciated. Thank you.

Finally, my sincere appreciation goes out to all those on the Chevy Performance Team with whom I talked. Thank you all.

Jim Campbell,
U.S. VP of Performance Vehicles and Motorsports

Sandor Piszar,
Director, Chevrolet Performance

Dr. Jamie Meyer,
Performance Marketing Manager

Roger Allen,
COPO Assembly Manager, Chevrolet Racing

Cliff Cohen,
Marketing Manager, Chevy Performance,
Service and Parts

Steve Johnson,
COPO Assistant Program Manager

Mark Kent,
Director, Chevrolet Racing

Jeff Kettman,
Purchasing Manager, Chevrolet Racing

Russ O'Blenes,
Manager, GM Racing Powertrains

Al Oppenheiser,
Camaro Chief Engineer

Tom Read,
Assistant Manager, GM Technology Communications

David Ross,
GM Design

Robin Wright,
COPO Program Manager

And to those who provided information, assistance and insight:

Jim Boburka,
Jim Crivelli Chevrolet

Ernie Callard,
GM Performance Parts Division, retired

Victor Cagnazzi,
Cagnazzi Racing

Paul J. Cambria,
Attorney at Law

Dave Connolly,
driver, Cagnazzi Racing

John Gibson,
Detroit Public Library

Rick Hendrick,
Hendrick Motorsports and
Hendrick Automotive Group

Bill Howell,
GM Engineering, retired

Ralph Kramer,
Chevrolet Public Relations, retired

Paige Plant,
Automotive History Collection,
Detroit Public Library

Mike Pustelny,
owner, MPR Race Cars

Eric Reyes,
driver, Jimmy Vasser Chevrolet

Rich Rinke,
owner, Turn Key Automotive

Jim Vasser Sr.,
Jimmy Vasser Chevrolet

And to my colleagues and friends on the *Automobile Quarterly* team:

Kaye Bowles-Durnell	John Durnell
Dan Bulleit	Tim Lee
Michelle Donahue	Jennifer Harrington
Michelle Houtsch	Sara Lardé
Deb Murphy	Greg Perigo
Deb Poag	Roy Poag
Ronny Seals	

Finally, I would like to thank GM Designer David Ross for providing the incredible renderings in Chapter Nine. They truly add historical documentation. Throughout the project, I often remembered what David told me:

"As a lifelong enthusiast and drag racer, working on a project like the COPO Camaro is one of those career moments you dream about. Truly, few cars can go really fast and look really good!"

Looking really good.

Going really fast.

That, in a nutshell, is what the COPO Camaro is all about.

Jeffrey K. Leestma
September 2012

Photo Credits:

General Motors: Pages 6, 13-15, 21, 28 (Pace Car), 30, 38-49, 56, 59, 60, 89 (bottom), 94

Automobile Quarterly Archives: Pages 4 (Louis Chevrolet), 8-12, 16-20, 22-29, 31-33, 36-37

Jeffrey K. Leestma: Pages 64 (bottom), 74, 76-78, 79 (inset), 80-84, 86, 87, 88 (right), 89 (top), 90 (left), 96, 103, 108-113, 151, 153, 156 (top), 157

Mike Pustelny/MPR Race Cars: 62, 63, 64 (top), 65-73

Dave DeSmythers/R.J. Conlin, Inc.: Rear cover (large image), Title page, Pages 4, 52-55, 61, 111, 172

Mark Kelly/MPK Photo: Pages 75, 79, 81 (throttle body inlet), 85, 88 (left), 90 (right), 91-93

Auto Imagery, Inc.: Rear cover (insets). Pages 50, 150, 152, 154, 155, 156 (bottom), 158, 159

Jim Boburka: Front cover, Page 3

Dana Mecum: 34, 35

Justin Cesler, GM High-Tech Performance: Page 58

PUSH
OFF